Brian. W

CW01650028

I E

WILD PIG

For those who survive against the odds

BY THE SAME AUTHOR

Fiction
Fawn
Stag
White Patch
Razorback

Non-fiction
Pack and Rifle
Hunter by Profession
Backblocks
The Deer Hunters
Seasons of a Hunter
The Hunting Breed
Outdoors in Australia
On Target
The Wild Pig in New Zealand
The Golden Years of Hunting in New Zealand
The Golden Years of Fishing in New Zealand
New Zealand: Hunters' Paradise
Holden on Hunting
The Deerstalkers
A Guide to Hunting in New Zealand
The Hunting Experience
Hunt South
Wild Game
More Holden on Hunting
Fall Muster
On the Routeburn Track
Along the Dingo Fence

IN SEARCH OF THE WILD PIG

PHILIP HOLDEN

Hodder & Stoughton
AUCKLAND LONDON SYDNEY TORONTO

In the weighing and measuring of game, imperial measurements are still used. For those more familiar with metric, the following conversions are applicable:

1 inch	25.4 millimetres
1 foot	0.3048 metre
1 pound	0.4536 kilogram

First published 1992
ISBN 0 340 575662

Typeset by Design Techniques Ltd, Auckland
Printed and bound in Hong Kong for
Hodder & Stoughton Ltd, 46 View Road,
Glenfield, Auckland, New Zealand

Contents

Author's Note

The wild pig is certainly the most widespread and numerous game animal in New Zealand today, with a range far overlapping that of the most common deer, the red. Wild pigs are found in varying densities from the very tip of the North Island to the bottommost parts of the South Island, and they are found on many offshore islands. All told they inhabit more than 28 percent of New Zealand's total landmass and well-established populations, always difficult to assess in number, are presently found within easy striking distance of every major city and town.

Wherever they are found, wild pigs are resourceful, hardy and highly intelligent. In a hostile world, where almost everyone is against them, they somehow continue to survive. Against overwhelming odds, wild pigs will often fight to the death. Fearlessly, they battle it out with much larger predators, particularly when defending their young. There is, I believe, much to admire about wild pigs.

A work of this type would be impossible to undertake unless the author was blessed with the cooperation of many people. I would like to thank, with the deepest appreciation, the following people.

Pig-hunters and members of pig-hunting clubs: Alan Lee, Allan Hampshire, Martin Spiers, Mike Hutchins, John Chaffey, R.W. Little, Gary Fox, Brett Millward, John Williamson, Graham Palamountain, Hans Brink, Kevin Henderson, Stuart Hewitt, Bob Pittaway, Bob Jeffares, Larry Wheal, Tom Newell, Peter Broughton, Lindsay Goudie, Colin Quinn, Brian 'Snow' Quinn, Ben Lucas, Sam Lucas, James Lucas, Hamish Cameron, Colin Ashmore, Ken Johnson and Willie 'Wong' Cowie.

On stations and farms: John 'Tussock' Lucas (Timburn), Cotty Burdon (Mount Burke), Jerry Burdon (Glen Dene), John Aspinall (Mount Aspiring), Peter and Ann Presland (Minaret), Denis Fastier (Queensberry Ridges) and Alan Gillespie.

The 'wild bunch': Darkie Duff, Keri Duff, Manu Edwards, Colin 'Bing'

Albert, Pat Tahi, Moss Albert and Manu Jensen.

Department of Conservation: Wanting to bring to public attention the grave consequences of liberating pigs in areas where they were not previously established, Department of Conservation personnel went out of their way to assist me, providing unpublished reports and letters and talking of their experiences. I thank profusely: Don Woodcock (Great Barrier Island), Don McKenzie (Whangarei), Kerry Matthews (New Plymouth), Peter Brady (Havelock), Bill Cash (Picton), Alan Jones (Tauranga), Carol Long (Tauranga), Roly Martin (ex-Queenstown), Bryne Barron (Queenstown), Paul Hondelink (Wanaka), John Fleming (Hawea), Terry Farrell (Hokitika), Peter Willemse (Invercargill), Andy Cox (Invercargill), Allan Munn (Chatham Islands), and Peter Hill and John Roberts, DoC hunters on Karioi Mountain, Raglan County in 1980.

Veterinary surgeons: Gary Walker (Wanaka) and Steve Mirams (Wellington).

MAF personnel: Owen Churchman, Russell Bryant and Gary Knowles at Alexandra.

I would also like to thank Val Johnson, Mike Davie, Barry Lanauze, Colin Clarke, Alan Duncan, Shereen Brink, Judy Ashmore, Shirley Hewitt, Stuart Devar and Dave Bragg.

The chapter 'A Matter of Anonymity' was only made possible because of the person who talked to me without hesitation about his part in liberating pigs in various parts of Central and Western Otago. For obvious reasons he is unnamed in the narrative. My heartfelt appreciation to him, too, for allowing me to add an extra and completely unexpected dimension to the book.

All photographs are my own.

Philip Holden
Queenstown, 1992

NORTH ISLAND

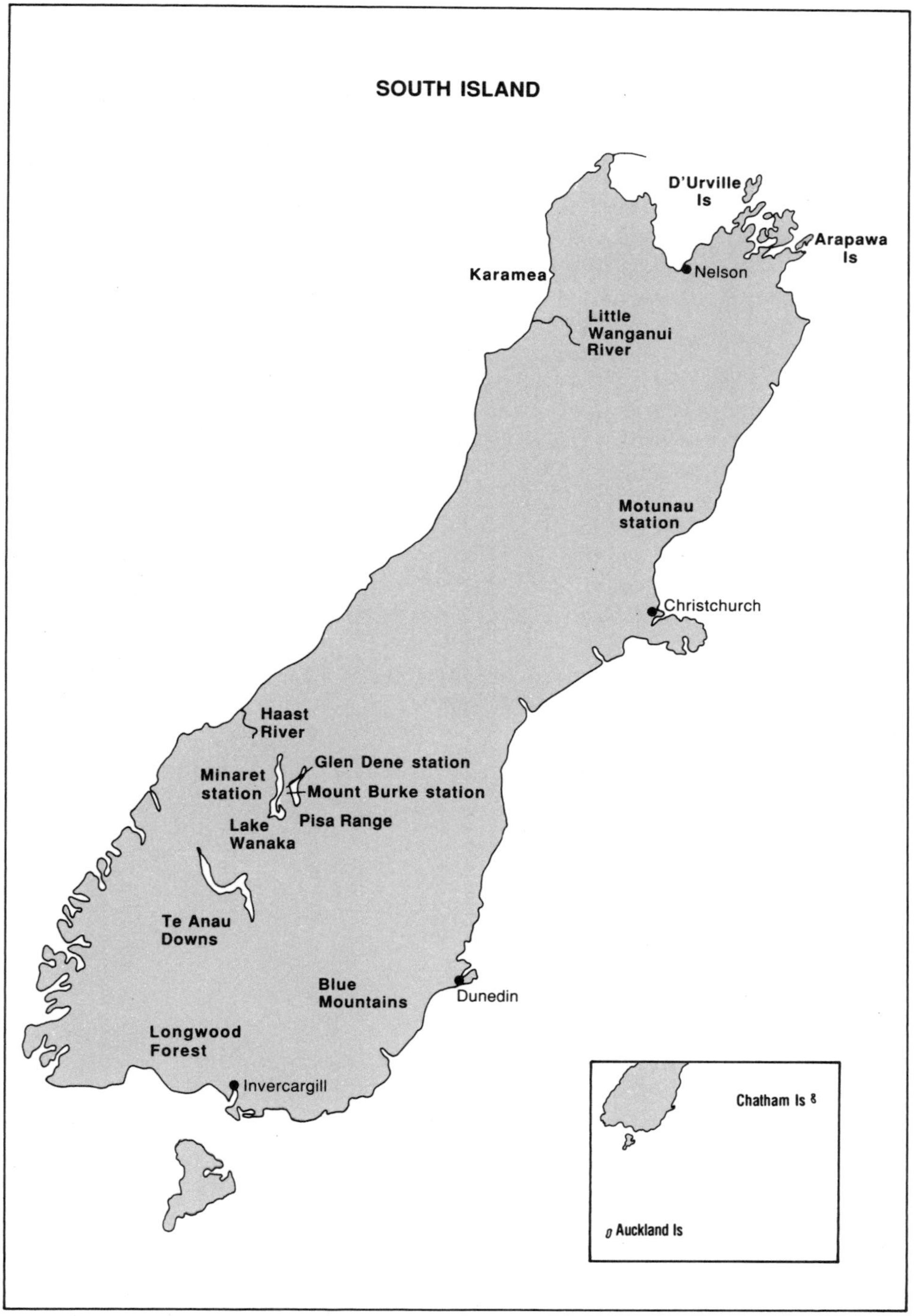

SOUTH ISLAND
D'Urville Is
Arapawa Is
Nelson
Karamea
Little Wanganui River
Motunau station
Christchurch
Haast River
Glen Dene station
Minaret station
Mount Burke station
Pisa Range
Lake Wanaka
Te Anau Downs
Blue Mountains
Dunedin
Longwood Forest
Invercargill
Chatham Is
Auckland Is

"There is a common view that pig hunting has become more popular in the last 15 years since deer hunting became less attractive as numbers declined. It is probably this change in emphasis that has lead to the attempts to liberate pigs to create new hunting areas."

Terry Farrell, Conservation Officer,
Wild Animal Control, Hokitika

PART ONE

To Liberate a Pig

Lee Rua Te Haara and a boar from the Hunua Range, near Auckland, spring 1983.

A World-wide Family of Pigs

The wild pigs of New Zealand are members of a family that is well represented in both the Old and the New World. They are classified as Suidae — meaning Old World pigs — and are the oldest and the most primitive of all the living even-toed ungulates. The Suidae comprise five genera, the most familiar being the genus *Sus*. This genus includes, among others, the European wild boar, the Indian wild boar, the domestic pig and the feral pig (reverted from domesticated to completely wild). The other genera are *Phacochoerus, Potamochoerus, Hylochoerus* and *Babirusa*.

There is little real difference between the wild boars — be they truly wild or feral — that range dense woods in Germany, arid regions in India, snow-bound forests in Siberia, humid islands in the Pacific Ocean, swampy river systems in Australia, and so many parts of New Zealand. The genus we are concerned with, *Sus*, is broken up into a number of subspecies, the most prominent of which is the European wild boar, which was the forerunner of most domestic breeds of pigs.

European wild boar *Sus scrofa scrofa*

The European wild boar was once common in England, Scotland and Wales, although it never got as far as Ireland. Relentless hunting, combined with a gradual reduction in its once almost unlimited range, inevitably resulted in the extinction of the species in Great Britain in the later part of the seventeenth century. For precisely the same reasons it would also die out in Sweden and Norway. Attempts in the 1880s to reintroduce the wild boar into Great Britain — mainly into enclosed parks — failed, although they were successfully re-established in Sweden and Norway.

On at least four separate occasions — in the 1890s, 1910, 1912 and 1925 — the European wild boar was introduced into the USA. The 1912 introduction is worth commenting on. An English sportsman, George

Gordon Moore, imported fourteen pigs — mostly boars — and turned them out into a 1500-acre (600-hectare) hunting reserve in the Appalachian Mountains of North Carolina. Initially, they were restricted to a special pen constructed of strong chestnut rails. There was much speculation about how they would react to the comparatively small enclosure. They were, of course, wild animals and what indignities they must have endured since being captured and transported by sea, train and bullock-drawn wagon. We may presume the boars were sick of being confined because, with awesome power, they attacked the fencing and, to a pig, broke free. In despair, George Gordon Moore watched them escape into the nearby forest. Soon, with typical pig audacity, the boars were mating at will with unpenned domestic stock and today an untold number of hybrid pigs inhabit some of the wildest terrain in North Carolina and Tennessee. Some of the boars grow to a huge size and are commonly referred to as the Russians, indicating precisely where Moore obtained the initial stock.

During the early 1930s, a number of 'Bavarian' wild boar were imported into several exotic forests in the south-western Cape of South Africa, to control the larvae of the pine tree emperor moth, which were defoliating the trees. The idea was that the pigs would root out the moths' pupae, which, among other things, they most successfully did. As with wild boar introduced into North America, they gradually intermixed with domestic stock and today their descendants provide hunters with grand sport and local authorities with all sorts of unwanted problems.

Apart from man, the main enemy of the European wild boar — in its traditional range — is the wolf. They are implacable enemies. Traditionally, wolves hunt in packs and therein lies their advantage — they simply outnumber their prey. A German forest warden once told of how he was able, by the sign he found, to reconstruct the pattern of a battle between one boar and five wolves. The wolves, of course, won, for the forest warden found the boar dead. It must have been an awesome battle, however, for there were five separate blood-stained tracks leading away from where the carcass of the valiant boar lay in the snow, indicating that each wolf had sustained injuries during the fight.

Today the wild boar is found in southern and central Europe, south of the Baltic Sea. The head and body may measure up to 71 inches, and the tail may add another 10–18½ inches. The European wild boar measures 36–40 inches at the shoulder. It has six incisors, a pair of canines and seven teeth in each half of the jaw; the canines extend, in the case of the boar, into significant tusks and constitute its principal weapon. The European wild boar may weigh up to a remarkable 750 pounds, for exceptionally large boars ranging the Carpathian Mountains of Poland, Czechoslovakia and Rumania.

Regarding size, the general trend appears to be that as the European wild boar spreads eastwards from its westernmost ranges it grows bigger; the same applies to red deer, too. The average weight for an adult male in

Germany is about 200 pounds, while in Turkey it is closer to 400 pounds, and in many parts of Russia they have been reported up to 600 pounds. In North America adult boars vary from 200 to 350 pounds. Almost always the heavier animals bear the most resemblance to the true wild boar — that is, they are of purer breeding.

The adult wild boar is characterised by a massive body and a distinctly triangular head, which extends into a significant snout. The shortish legs are slender, resulting in a minimal area of contact with the ground. Each limb terminates in four toes, of which only the two central ones actually grip the ground; the two less-developed lateral toes serve a vital purpose when the animal is in swampy terrain, where, in the manner of webbed feet, they help to prevent it sinking and drowning.

The overall shape of a pig's body is an evolutionary adaptation to its mostly forested habitat and allows it to move with speed through the heaviest undergrowth, which is invaluable when an Asian tiger, a pack of European wolves, or a hunter's team of blood-hungry dogs is on the hunt for an adversary that in India has been known to kill a fully grown tiger by disembowelling it with an upward slash of its formidable tusks.

The wild boar is suitably attired for its varied environment. The pelage consists mostly of coarse bristles, mixed with some much finer hair. The overall effect follows no set pattern and may be grey, blackish, brown or variegated, and is often quite striking. In winter, and depending on precisely where they range, they may grow a thick woolly underfur.

The very young — called squeakers — are characterised by a short snout and alternating light and dark brown bands along the length of the back; the hair has yet to coarsen and is of a silk-like texture. At six months of age the stripes start to fade and a year later they are attired in their final coat.

Indian wild boar *Sus scrofa cristatus*

This is a larger animal than its European counterpart, standing a full 40–41 inches at the shoulder and weighing as much as 360 pounds. The Indian wild boar has long been hunted from horseback and it is generally believed that the sport of pig-sticking became popular in India when the bear became scarce. British cavalrymen, serving in India in the early part of the nineteenth century, enthusiastically took to pig-sticking, using a lance rather than the traditional Indian spear. Pig-sticking, which is still popular in India but no longer practised in Europe, was carried out in New Zealand during the last century and, according to T. E. Donne (1924), even into the current one.

The Indian wild boar varies in colour from a reddish-brown to black, often, in darker animals, intermingled with white. In warmer areas it may be almost devoid of hair and in cooler areas quite thickly coated. The Indian wild boar is found throughout India, Burma and Sri Lanka. A number of almost indefinable subspecies of *Sus scrofa cristatus* inhabit

Thailand, Vietnam, Cambodia, the Malay Peninsula, and numerous islands where natives have constantly transplanted their domestic stock, which, invariably, have interbred with the local wild strain.

An interesting point concerning boars that inhabit regions where rattan palms grow, mainly in the East Indies, is that they are among the few wild animals in the world that will attack humans without provocation. It is thought that as they forage under the rattan palms (a climbing palm with long, thin, jointed, pliable stems) they pick up needle-like thorns and become increasingly short-tempered, particularly when the tiny wounds become infected.

◦ ◦ Chinese wild pig *Sus scrofa moupinensis*
Two very distinct types of this strain of *Sus scrofa* are found: black with a few whitish hairs and reddish-brown with a more than generous sprinkling of black. They range central China, from the coast to western Kansu and Szechuan. A number of lesser subspecies occur further north and in a few parts of southern China.

◦ ◦ Andaman wild pig *Sus scrofa andamanensis*
This shaggy-coated pig with brownish-grey bristles along its back ranges the forests of the Andaman Islands (a union territory of India) and, specifically, two islands in the Bay of Bengal.

◦ ◦ Barbary wild boar *Sus scrofa barbarus*
A pig that is a little smaller and darker than its European cousin, this lives in a generally warmer climate, so its coat is shorter and much less dense. The name Barbary refers to its habitat, the western part of north Africa: the heavily forested mountains of Algeria, Tunisia and Morocco.

◦ ◦ Pygmy hog *Sus salvanius*
Since a fully grown adult reaches a height of about twelve inches at the shoulder, it comes as no surprise to learn this is the smallest of all wild pigs. Normally it is two-toned: black and brown. Its range is the swampy grasslands along the southern borders of north-west Assam, and the forests of Nepal, Sikkim and Bhutan. The pygmy hog, never plentiful in numbers and about which very little is known, may well be extinct today; in recent years there have been no reliable reports of its being sighted.

◦ ◦ Bornean wild pig (bearded pig) *Sus barbatus barbatus*
This animal is similar in height to the European wild boar; it is characterised by a rather high-ridged narrow frame and a greatly elongated head. Black in colour, with few variations, its cheeks have a thick beard, hence its alternative name. A warty outgrowth, covered with stiff bristles, is considerably more prominent in males. Its range is Borneo, the

Malay Peninsula and Sumatra. It was introduced to the Philippines via Palawan.

- Javan warty pig *Sus verrocosus*
Another two-toned (black and brown) pig with a small crest of lighter brown hair on the crown and a distinct whitish patch of hair on either side of the jaw. It is a medium to small animal with three distinct warts on each side of its face, the largest being just under the eye. Its range is Java and Papua New Guinea via, it is thought, the Lesser Sunda and Maluku Islands. *Sus verrocosus* and *Sus scrofa* are quite compatible and, consequently, they have interbred in Papua New Guinea.

- Celebes wild pig *Sus celebensis*
Closely related to the Jarvan warty pig, this is a smallish animal with black hair and a white buff line extending over the nose, just below the eyes, and continuing from the corner of the mouth to a white patch of hair on the cheek. A single, smallish wart is located between the eye and nose. It is found in Sulawesi (formerly the Celebes Islands) and was introduced, in a semi-feral state, on the island of Buru, east of Borneo.

- Philippine wild pig *Sus philippensis*
This is a medium to small pig with sparse black hair; a few brown and white hairs grow on the forehead and on the upper neck and a small clump of whitish hair on either side of the jaw is not uncommon. It is found on a number of islands in the Philippines.

- Domestic pig *Sus domestica*
Some scientists are of the opinion that pigs were first domesticated in the neolithic era, some 6500 years ago; a Chinese scholar has estimated that his people domesticated the pig about 2900 BC. It is quite likely that the pig was used initially as a scavenger, before it was discovered how good its flesh was to eat. Certainly the early Egyptians, Romans and Greeks all realised the advantages of raising pigs for meat: they were comparatively easy to raise in captivity, could be fed virtually anything, and very little of the carcass was wasted.
In the time of the Saxons, pigs were held in high esteem. An illustration in Queen Mary's Psalter (1310) depicts swineherds knocking acorns off oak trees for pigs to feed on, and the pigs are shown as long legged, hairy, razor backed. The wild boar was, of course, still comparatively common in many parts of Great Britain then.
Scientific breeding of pigs commenced in the eighteenth century when pigs from east and south-east Asia were brought to Europe and crossed with local versions. Today there are over 300 domestic breeds or local varieties of pigs scattered throughout the world. The entire pig or hog population is approximately 750 million, with as many as 40 percent being

found in China. The former Soviet Union ranked second in pig production, with the USA in third place.

Farmers all over the world raise pigs; the advantages of doing so are many. The meat is consumed in a variety of ways: chops, loin roasts, spare ribs, ham, bacon and sausage. Lard used for cooking is made of pig fat. Some religions, such as Islam and Judaism, strictly forbid the consumption of pork.

Tanneries process the skins of pigs into leather, which in turn is used in the making of clothing, belts, gloves and shoes. The stiff hair of the pig provides bristles for brushes, and is used to stuff mattresses and baseball mitts and to make insulating materials. Pig blood is used in the manufacture of fertiliser, animal feeds and medicines. Pharmaceutical companies use pig glands to make insulin and other medicines. As well as lard, pig fat is also made into soap, candles, salves, shaving cream, explosives and lubricating oils. The bones of the pig are ground down for glue, fertiliser, animal feeds and bone oil.

Such a broad diversity of uses of a pig's carcass must surely make it unique among domesticated animals.

◦ ◦ Red river hog *Potamochoerus porcus porcus*

Considered a subspecies of bush pig, this is perhaps the most striking of all wild pigs. Found mostly near water (it is an excellent swimmer), the red river hog is a medium-sized pig, bright orange-red in colour with distinctive black and white markings on the face, long tufts of white on the ends of the ears, a white crest along the spine, and a long tail. In old age males may turn black.

Red river hogs often force tunnels through heavy undergrowth and, using their shoulders and backs, lever up interlocked vegetation to form effective roofs over their dens. Like other pigs they are gregarious, living in groups of up to twenty. Older boars, however, may decide to live in isolation. The range of the red river hog is western Africa, particularly Equatorial Guinea; close relatives are found in Cameroon, Liberia and Congo.

◦ ◦ South African bush pig *Potamochoerus porcus koiropotamus*

Standing in excess of thirty inches at the shoulder, and weighing up to 200 pounds, the bush pig is well covered with coarse hair, most males being blackish-brown in colour, with females tending more to brown inter-mixed with grey.

Like other pigs, they are omnivorous, but given the choice they seem to prefer vegetation. A farmer's crops are always in favour where the bush pig is concerned and, under cover of night, they gain access to maize or potato crops by burrowing under fences or, if that is not possible, by snapping the wires. Not even a barbed-wire fence will stop a determined bush pig.

The range is south-eastern Africa. A smaller but very similar cousin, the Madagascar bush pig (*Potamochoerus porcus larvatus*) is found only on the island of Madagascar, where, in the north, it poses a continual threat to the gravely endangered Malagasy tortoise.

∘ ∘ Forest hog *Hylochoerus meinertzhageni*

This is the largest of African pigs and it is a big animal by any standards, standing up to 40 inches at the shoulder and weighing up to 500 pounds. Generally speaking, the forest hog is a heavy-set, blackish-grey pig with a somewhat scanty coat of stiff hairs (the skin may show through the hairs). It has a heavy wart below the eye and a distinct tuft at the end of a long tail; it bears a marked resemblance to the much better-known warthog of the African plains, which is its nearest relative.

Like the red river hog, it tunnels extensively in dense underbrush, creating linking pathways that lead to huge communal dens occupied by families for generations. Unlike the red river hog, however, it seldom digs or roots, but feeds on leaves, grasses and, should the opportunity arise, small birds and mammals.

The male forest hog is known for his aggressive nature, especially when protecting his territory or his family. He may charge without warning and that might prove fatal, for he may grow tusks that protrude from his lower jaw for a good nine inches.

The forest hog can be found in high-altitude forests, as a rule, from Kenya and Tanzania through Congo to Cameroon.

∘ ∘ Warthog *Phacochoerus aethiopicus*

Easily the most recognisable of the African pigs (because of the numbers of times it has been featured on television), the warthog derives its name from two very prominent warts on either side of its face. An adult may reach 34 inches at the shoulder, have a length of 60 inches and weigh 330 pounds. The normal colour is a blackish-grey; like the forest hog, it is sparsely covered with bristly hairs, so the skin is exposed. A heavy mane extends down the back and on either side of the body. The tail is well tufted. Oddly enough, the young, in contrast with other pigs, are not striped at birth.

While some consider the warthog an ugly and ferocious-looking customer, the truth is that they are by nature rather friendly souls, forming lasting family attachments. Living on the hot plains means they have many natural enemies, such as lions, cheetahs and leopards. Because of this they have been given the most impressive fighting weapons of any member of the family of pigs. Record tusks may measure 24 inches, but a more normal set will be around 10–12 inches.

Most predators, with a plump young warthog in mind for supper, think twice before committing themselves to attack. They know that the young are almost always under strict control, close to a watchful adult. A sudden charge to take an unsuspecting young warthog will result, almost certainly, in a reaction of untold fury. Of course, many young and adult warthogs are taken by carnivores — especially by lions operating in packs — but they are often able to drive away a cheetah or leopard or even a lion operating on its own. Pound for pound there is no animal on the African continent that can fight so fiercely and so effectively. The same trait is, of course, alive in the wild boar wherever it is found.

◦ ◦ Babirusa *Babirusa babirusa*

There are apparently two forms of this medium-to-large pig, one found on the large island of Sulawesi (formerly called Celebes) and the other on the island known as Togian. The former (*B. b. celebensis*) is almost bald, its creased skin slate grey. The latter is sparsely covered with greyish hair. Either way, the males grow extremely large tusks, second in size only to those of the warthog.

The babirusa is a real puzzle. It has, for instance, two stomachs; and like a cow chews its cud. Indeed, its Malay name suggests something enigmatic: 'babi' means pig, 'rusa' means deer. In its dense rainforest habitat the babirusa eats like a sheep, runs like a deer, and can swim like a champion.

Today the babirusa is possibly endangered, the main reason being that tribesmen believe that its tusks hold special magic powers. The flesh of this pig is considered a delicacy (a report in a United States Agency for International Development publication in 1985 said the babirusa might be a kosher pig whose meat could be eaten by Jews and Muslims). Despite the fact that the Indonesian government has placed the babirusa on the protected list, hunting still goes on. In 1986 a team of zoologists was unable to find any traces of the babirusa in Sulawesi's deep rainforests. Prior to the 1970s the babirusa roamed here freely in large numbers. The babirusa has been liberated on the island of Buru, east of Sulawesi.

◦ ◦ Peccary *Tayassus tajacu*

Also known as javelina or musk pig, peccaries differ from true pigs for a number of reasons and have been separated into a specific family, Tayassuidae. Differences include their upper, dagger-like tusks, which are directed straight downwards rather than upwards and outwards, their one lateral hoof (or dew-claw) on each hind leg, and their small, raised, practically functionless lateral hooves. Also, they have a large musk gland on the back, about eight inches from the tail. Like the babirusa's, the peccary's litter rarely exceeds two.

While various forms of peccary exist, there are two main types. Generally speaking, they are sturdy, compact animals standing up to 25 inches at the shoulder and weighing around 65 pounds. The collared peccary, which is found from the south-west of the USA through to

Patagonia, is tawny and black, appearing grizzled or speckled, with a light grey collar and white lip or chin. In Costa Rica, the collared peccary has a tawny, instead of lighter, collar. The white-lipped peccary, found from Mexico to Paraguay, is less tawny and more black, and is slightly larger. Lesser forms are found in the low forested region of Honduras, in north-western Mexico, and in Paraguay and northern Argentina.

The Consequences of Liberation

Pigs are the most adaptable animals in the world. Domesticated pigs that have been liberated and have reverted to a feral state, and none does so more quickly than pigs do, soon display the characteristics of a true wild boar. They will, for instance, grow much larger tusks — to be used not for digging but as weapons; their curly tails straighten, and may become much thicker at the end, like, say, a bushy fly swat; their hair thickens, becoming coarser. Often they will trim down, with the majority of their weight up front where it counts. When cornered or provoked they will mostly react with untold ferocity and admirable bravery.

Today, there are well-established populations of feral pigs in many parts of the world. They may be found in Norway and southern Sweden, South Africa and Sudan, eighteen states of mainland USA, many islands in the West Indies, Peru, Chile, Brazil, Colombia, Bolivia and Argentina, the Falkland Islands, Australia and New Zealand, many islands in Indonesia, including Enggano (where they apparently swam ashore following a nineteenth-century shipwreck), Malaysia, Papua New Guinea, Fiji, Hawaii, Mauritius, and numerous lesser-known islands.

This is not a definitive account of the distribution of the feral pig throughout the world, but, interestingly enough, when all of these regions are added to the broad range of the wild boar it makes it seem possible that the wild pig is the most widely distributed game animal in the world.

A classic example of a pig's ability to adapt to a wide variety of habitats can be found in Jamaica, where today's feral stock are directly descended from animals introduced by the Spanish in the late fifteenth century and, partly, from domestic pigs abandoned by slaves following the abolition of slavery. Here, surrounded by the Caribbean Sea, pigs occupy a habitat that ranges from brackish, humidity-ridden swamps at sea level, to the arid south coast, right up to the almost perpetually wet montane forest at altitudes of up to 2000 metres.

The wild pig will eat virtually anything it encounters, and this is perhaps the main reason why it survives where more selective species would simply die out. Given its omnivorous nature and its intelligence, a pig is an animal to reckon with. To maintain its food supply it has teeth like chisels, capable of inflicting a ghastly bite, jaws that resembled a powerful vice, and an exaggerated snout that is hard and is linked by a pre-nasal bone to a very muscular neck and shoulders. The result is a perfectly designed lever that allows a pig, with little apparent effort, to break up hard-packed earth and to shatter by sheer persistence partly rotted logs wherein many tempting grubs may lie.

A pig is a most thorough chewer of its food. Interestingly enough, it will also eat the dung of other animals — if the situation is critical enough to demand it. Like domestic fowl, it has been observed to eat cow manure. A pig is able to do this because of its unique digestive system, built for survival in the harshest circumstances, which allows it to find a source of food in what others have passed through their bodies and rejected. Indeed, should a pig be confined to a yard and fed nothing but a very limited amount of grain, it will eat any faeces that contain undigested grain.

In Australia feral pigs kill and eat venomous snakes. From this one might suspect they are naturally immune to the effects of snake bite, but in fact they rely for immunity on a rather thick layer of adipose tissue directly under the skin. Also, like the snake-killing mongooses of India, they possess faster muscular movements than a snake; it is thought pigs kill snakes by trampling them with their sharp hooves.

As a rule a sow is ready to breed at around eight to ten months old. The gestation period is thought to be about the same for both wild and domestic pigs — about four months. In the course of a year a sow may have two litters, depending, of course, on whether or not conditions are favourable. There is no particular breeding season for feral pigs, so a sow may give birth at any time of the year. Because of the warmer weather, however, when there is a much lower mortality rate among new-born pigs, one is more likely to observe a sow with young in the spring and early summer. Having said that, I have observed a sow with a new brood in the middle of winter.

A sow is equipped with twelve teats; she may give birth to that number of piglets; she may, and very often does in a domestic situation, far exceed it. An exceptional litter could number eighteen; a rare one as many as twenty-four. Naturally not all survive. In the wild it is entirely different: a sow, for some unknown reason, has a much more modest brood to look out for. A likely number is six to eight, with seven the most common. Higher and lower numbers are often observed in the wild, however. Even if only half of each litter reaches breeding age (males are ready to mate at around one year old), feral pigs, given the right circumstances, can easily increase their numbers tenfold in a comparatively short space of time.

In 1493, Christopher Columbus liberated pigs in the West Indies. They found the locale ideal and multiplied accordingly. Not only that, they reverted to a wild state so readily that a mere thirteen years later mobs of pigs were killing cattle. The islanders responded by hunting and killing those responsible. In 1539 thirteen pigs were liberated in Florida and just three years later they were said to number 700. Today feral pigs are present in sixty-six of Florida's sixty-seven counties.

Pigs were also liberated as a source of food for sealers, whalers, or any poor unfortunates who, because of shipwreck, might have found themselves scratching for a decent feed on a remote island. Kangaroo Island, off the coast of South Australia, is a case in point. In 1803 Frenchman Nicolas Baudin liberated pigs there and within twenty years they were so abundant that one of the island's inlets was named Hog Bay.

In 1820 the cutter *Princess of Wales* went aground on Ile aux Cochons (Pig Island), in the Indian Ocean. Her captain, C. M. Goodridge, wrote about the incident and the numbers of pigs there in his *Narrative of a Voyage to the South Seas*, published in 1834. The pigs, he said, were 'very numerous and very ferocious' on Ile aux Cochons and they fed mainly on the roots of tussock grasses and on sea-birds, particularly penguins. Naturally enough, Ile aux Cochons became a popular spot for sealers to replenish their meat supplies — salted down pork, we may presume, was a specialty. Sir James Clark Ross wrote that, despite the best efforts of the sealers, in 1840 'you could hardly land for [pigs]'.

In Hawaii pigs, which are thought to have arrived there with the Polynesian colonists in about AD 1000, are numerous. They cause significant damage in native forest areas, mainly by rooting up seedlings. They are also held responsible for the near demise of the Hawaiian goose and the dark-rumped petrel. Pigs were liberated on the island of Mauritius by a Portuguese seaman, Pedro Mascarenhas, in 1512. Among the ground-nesting birds harmed by the liberation was a very large flightless bird. The dodo fared particularly badly and by the late seventeenth century was extinct.

Shortly after the Spanish explorer Juan de Bermudez discovered the Bermuda Islands in 1515, pigs were liberated there as, again, a potential food supply for shipwrecked mariners. In 1609 English Admiral Sir George Somers was wrecked there and recorded that 'our people in the Bermudas found such abundance of hogs that for nine months' space they plentifully sufficed and yet the number seemed not diminished'. It is worth pointing out that when the Spanish took control of the Bermudas the Bermuda petrel is estimated to have numbered in excess of one million. A century later, naturalists, stunned by the damage the prolific feral pig was causing, considered they had gradually reduced the population to around 100,000 birds.

Pigs were released on the Galapagos Islands in about 1832. They have been particularly severe on both the giant tortoise and the East Pacific green turtle populations. Typically, they uproot the nests and feed on the eggs; with uncanny instinct, they also seem to know precisely when the hatchlings are making their way to the surface and move in for the kill. Pigs are reckoned to cause a thirty percent reduction in the annual populations of both species. The birds to suffer pig predation on the Galapagos Islands include the American race of the greater flamingo, the Galapagos dove and the dark-rumped petrel. The Galapagos pigs make life hazardous for both land and marine iguana. On Santiago Island, which is said to carry a feral pig population of around 20,000, almost every iguana nest on Espumilla Beach is attacked, usually within days after the iguanas begin laying.

The giant monitor lizard, known as the Komodo dragon, is found on a few small islands over 1500 kilometres east of Jakarta. In 1989 wildlife officers on Komodo Island, aware that the lizards were facing extinction, put out meat for them in special places. Naturally enough, the pigs found out and soon they were fighting the Komodo dragons over the handout. The dragons did not come out on top.

On the Tokelau Islands pigs often find that their food supply is limited, so they have turned to the sea as a source of sustenance. The pig is an excellent swimmer, quite capable of crossing tidal rivers; this most resourceful of animals wades and swims out through the shallow reef waters, constantly ducking its head to feed on sea slugs and shellfish.

The French explorer Louis Antoine de Bougainville introduced pigs to the Falkland Islands in 1764. A year later Commodore John Byron, leader of a British venture, also landed pigs at Port Egmont. Later, pigs were liberated as an emergency food source for whalers and sealers on various lesser islands in the Falklands, namely Bleaker, Beaver, New, Quaker, Speedwell and West Point. The pigs did well and soon reached feral status. Pig-hunting became very popular among the islanders, for the skins could be exported; in 1838 about 3000 pig skins were sent to Great Britain. By then huge areas of tussock land had been devastated by pigs, spelling disaster for the Magellan penguins, wild fowl, waders and petrels that had used the grasslands for shelter and nesting.

Particularly strong concentrations of feral pigs are found today in Brazil, especially in parts of the Mato Grosso, on the Bolivian border, and in the Llanos Orientale region of Colombia. In parts of Argentina they have interbred with the European wild boar, initially brought there in 1906 by ranch-holder Pedro Luro. There are European wild boar in the states of Santa Catarina and Parana in Brazil, where they have again hybridised with the feral pig.

Today the most numerous of the feral ungulates in North America is — not surprisingly — the pig. They are plentiful in the south-eastern and south-western states, where they are reckoned in their hundreds of thousands. Significantly, in some states, pigs have gained game animal status; the annual harvest in Florida and California is about 100,000 animals. Without such control measures, and even allowing for a 90 percent mortality rate among young animals, it is thought the overall population could increase by as much as 33 percent annually. Pigs compete with native American wildlife for a valuable supply of their food: nuts. This is a particular problem in the vast hardwood forests of California, where species to suffer include black bear, racoon, wild turkey, squirrel and, hardest hit of all, white-tailed deer. The wild boar in Europe regards nuts as a true delicacy, be they acorns or chestnuts and, using its lips and teeth, as sensitive as those of a female saltwater crocodile when handling her young, has no difficulty in removing the husk from the shell of even the smallest nuts.

While pigs have a broad range in Australia, it is in Queensland that they do the most damage. Pigs are estimated to cost the state tens of millions of dollars annually. This most pernicious of pests (which is how they are mostly regarded in Queensland) is judged guilty of, among other crimes, preying on lambs (as high as 30 percent in some years), calves, foals, poultry and bogged or injured animals. They damage 'vermin-proof' fences, a classic example being Queensland's 2500-kilometre section of the 5309-kilometre dingo fence known as the Barrier Fence. In regions of low to virtually no rainfall they wreck tanks, dams and water troughs, which is very often fatal to stock. They also feed heavily on vegetable crops, stored grain and hay, and cause untold damage in sugar cane and banana plantations.

Because of the hunting pressure, many Queensland pigs have moved to the cooler mountainous regions, where food is abundant and hunters are few. Once again, this most adaptable of animals, more likely descended from the Eurasian than the European wild boar, is proving second to none in the survival stakes.

Rampage!

In New Zealand the feral pig began to make a terrible nuisance of itself a very long time ago; it was in fact hunted both from sheer necessity and for sporting purposes long before the first red deer reached these shores. In 1867 von Hochsetter wrote:

> Cattle and swine run wild in various districts of the islands, and it is astonishing to what numbers the wild pigs are multiplying. They find an excellent and everywhere plentiful food in the fern-roots, which formerly served the Maoris as a chief article of food. They retire shyly from the immediate vicinity of the settlements, because the settlers hunt them down energetically; but they congregate in the yet uninhabited valleys in enormous numbers. The Wangapeka Valley in the Province of Nelson I saw for miles up and down literally ploughed up by thousands of wild pigs. They are nearly all black . . . Three men in twenty months, upon an area of 250,000 acres [100,000 hectares] killed not less than 25,000 of them.

The feral pig was considered directly responsible for the near-extinction of the tuatara, and for a telling reduction of the populations of ground-nesting birds, such as the kakapo, which, until te poaka ('the porker') arrived on the scene, had been undisturbed.

On the subantarctic Auckland Islands, where they were first liberated on the main island in 1807, pigs were, of course, up to their old tricks: digging up the burrows of nesting petrels, devouring the eggs and young of albatrosses and shags, and, with the able assistance of the feral cat, damaging the populations of the yellow-eyed penguin and the Auckland Island flightless teal. Native plant life also suffered. Grubbing tactics came in useful on the Chatham Islands, where, apart from giving birds a miserable time during the nesting period, they all but eliminated two endemic plants: the Chatham Island lily and *Aciphylla traversii*.

Wild pigs had a field day when many exotic forests were first established. Kaingaroa Forest, in the central North Island, was, in the depression-ridden 1930s, very much a case in point. Pigs were abundant in that country and they were particularly severe on Douglas fir and Corsican pine during the initial growth period.

Obviously, runholders had by this time become heartily sick of *Sus scrofa*, not that any of them called pigs that. Lambs had always been particularly vulnerable; so, too, were a farmer's crops. The consequences of liberating pigs into an environment they were never intended for is graphically illustrated in the following two stories.

A family called Byrch took over Motunau station on the north Canterbury coast in 1906. As a matter of interest, this was the first sheep station in the South Island, the run being taken up by the Greenwood brothers in 1846. Wild pigs were rampant in the area then and by 1906 nothing had changed. In fact, wild pigs were the biggest single problem the Byrches had to face.

Mostly the pigs on Motunau resided in large areas of manuka and gorse, the largest of which would soon become known as the Happy Valley block (later a part of Cheviot Hills station), away to the north of their homestead. The gorse and manuka provided excellent shelter; it was just too thick, too thorny, to hunt successfully. Even dogs shied away from it. The pigs, of course, made linking tunnels, their thick-hided skins more than adequate protection.

The Byrches decided to grow crops, among them, oats. Obviously they did not know how much pigs like oats. Pigs will travel long distances to feed on oats; they leave their daytime retreats in the late evening or just after dark, and make their way to ripening oat crops. Such overnight forays are carried out with admirable panache.

It is interesting to note that pigs reveal their intellectual ability when confronted with, say, a cereal crop that has attained maximum growth and the ripe ears are too high for them to reach. One might expect they would simply break off stalks one by one, the way a goat would. Pigs, however, are much smarter than goats and they trample down a small, roughly circular patch of oats and then scoop them up in tight bundles.

Pigs are really clued-up when the annual corn harvest comes around, too. They arrive under cover of darkness, moving with confidence behind enemy lines, scenting, listening, but mostly going on their gut instincts. There is much scattered corn upon the ground, but they ignore it. This is harvest time and the corn has been bagged, ready to be transported. A quick slash of tusks, a tearing bite, and corn spills out until the sack is quite empty. Lovely times for pigs and real bad news for farmers.

For the Byrches, then, pigs proved a major problem. Potentially high-earning oat crops were ruined and sacks of corn were torn open. The story goes that on one occasion a general hand, stacking sacks of corn, just happened to jab his pitchfork into one of the bags. Next moment, the entire stack collapsed and out of it, with the pitchfork firmly embedded in his rump, dashed a highly shocked boar!

The Byrches decided the best way to deal with the pigs would be to systematically fire the manuka and gorse. The unsuspecting pigs, fleeing ahead of the flames, would run into a steady stream of lead fired by waiting riflemen. The method worked well. If the wind suddenly changed — a southerly giving way to a raging northerly airblast — the pigs were in deep trouble. They could either stay and be burned alive or smash through a sheet of flames. Some pigs did break through the flames and escaped the bullets of the riflemen. Others were not as lucky and were turned to charred pork. Later, musterers would come across dazed pigs wandering around; every single hair had been scorched off their bodies, and some were blind.

In time, the Crown took over much of this pig-infested coastal land. The country was gradually broken in, and the pigs were slowly reduced by local hunters (some of whom are said to have shot hundreds) as their once impregnable habitat was eliminated.

Waireka station can be found way out beyond Raupunga in northern Hawke's Bay at the end of a secondary road. The station dates to 1881, when M. R. Miller took up 2400 hectares of freehold land together with 3200 hectares of Education Department land. Miller was more of a land speculator than anything else, and by the late 1880s he had sold out to Tom Caswell. He energetically set about turning the property into a paying proposition. First he purchased 1200 hectares of adjacent country in the Waiau River watershed, then another 800 hectares north of Mangaone. Gradually, Caswell increased stock numbers to 16,000 sheep; cattle were introduced and a woolshed was built. Some fencing was carried out, but mostly the land remained unfenced; its western and north-western boundaries were pure native forest that stretched without open tops for mile after mile.

The Maori of this region — Tuhoe — had had a long association with the pig, keeping them in a semi-wild state, much as the Aboriginal kept the dingo in pre-European times. The Maori hunted the pig for meat and, one would suspect, for sport, too. Eventually there were wild pigs through the length and breadth of the Urewera country, which, many years later in 1954, became a national park of 230,000 hectares.

Herein lay the problem on Waireka: there was nothing to stop untold numbers of pigs moving out of the forested country and onto newly cultivated pastures, to attack sickly ewes (no real loss) and newly born lambs (a real tragedy) with ferocity. Lambing time is, of course, the tail-end of winter, the start of spring. By September most sows are pregnant or have already given birth. Like a pregnant woman, a pregnant sow has special cravings, not the least of which is calcium, which is absolutely vital for the formation of bones and teeth. Once a sow has given birth it is also essential that a generous dose of calcium is contained in her milk if her piglets are to grow up strong and healthy. A sow has to seek out her own source of calcium and, instinctively, she will find it in a new-born lamb. A lamb is there for the taking: unlike most mothers, a ewe is incapable of any resistance. At lambing the wild pig is revealed for exactly what it is, a ruthless predator.

The turn of the century saw no respite from pig predation. If anything, it grew worse. By overburning and overgrazing humans left the way open for manuka, kanuka and fern to take a stranglehold, providing pigs with excellent habitat.

The period 1920–60 was, perhaps, the worst for New Zealand pigs, and the large-scale poison operations of the late 1950s and early 1960s were the real turning point in the battle. Constantly within this forty-year period sheepmen waged war on this pest of national importance. They virtually lived with their flocks at lambing time — they had to. Lambing at Waireka in 1944 was particularly bad; the pigs had never seemed more intent on untold mayhem. Of 150 ewes that gave birth in the Bald Hill paddock, for instance, only one lamb survived.

In this kind of horrendous situation, when pigs are rampant, competition amongst them for lambs is intense. A pig is too much of an opportunist to wait until he comes across a lamb. Somehow, pigs can sense when a ewe is about to give birth, by smell, sixth sense, whatever. They wait nearby, sometimes working themselves into a tightly controlled fury, until the ewe starts to give birth. Then the pig acts. Jaws clamp like a powerful vice around whatever the pig can get a solid hold of. Then, with a firm grip of the lamb's slimy body, they tear it free, the terrified ewe shocked into immobility.

God helps those who help themselves, the saying goes. The act of taking a lamb — which, of course, still occurs frequently in this country — serves a purpose for a calcium-craving sow. It is her very best insurance for the future of not only her young but that of her truly incredible species.

On Offshore Islands

Feral pigs are present today on a number of islands in New Zealand waters. They are never more destructive than when they are in an isolated situation where there are ground-nesting birds. However, it is to the lasting credit of the species that pigs survive in habitats as varied as, for instance, the scoria of Mayor Island, off the sun-drenched east coast of the North Island, and the storm-lashed subantarctic Auckland Islands, approximately 320 kilometres south of Stewart Island.

Great Barrier Island

Some 28,500 hectares in area, and located around 90 kilometres north-east of Auckland city, this is by far the largest of the North Island's offshore islands. One theory holds that Captain Cook liberated pigs on Great Barrier Island during his second voyage to New Zealand, to provide food for shipwrecked sailors, but the more popular belief is that the ancestors of the island's pig population, originally held as goods of trade, escaped from Ngatiwai or Ngatimaru. In the late 1970s feral pigs and goats were recognised as presenting a threat to the island's rare flora and fauna, and since then there have been attempts to eradicate the goats, and to reduce the numbers of pigs, through controlled recreational hunting. The pigs are hunted for food, although the odd large boar is kept as a trophy. Commercial hunting is not permitted on the DoC estate.

Mayor Island

This hilly, bush-clad, volcanic landmass of 1277 hectares, in the western Bay of Plenty, offers feral pigs a harsh lifestyle. Water is scarce and food far from plentiful; even foraging on a beach is ruled out because the generally rocky coastline offers few landing sites for incoming vessels. Pigs have been here for a long time — probably since the eighteenth century, when the island was a stronghold of the Ngaiterangi tribe.

Pigs survive here because of their versatility. They have to nose around rather than root because the ground is pumice and scoria. They turn over leaves, poking around the exposed root systems of such trees as rewarewa and pohutukawa. They make do. The population is thought to number no more than fifty, which is as many as the island can sustain. They are not big animals: a full-grown boar will not exceed 80 pounds live weight. Significantly, the pigs on Mayor Island are all black; it would appear that the original domesticated strain is untainted by subsequent liberations.

◦ ◦ Matakana Island

A hop, a step and a very big jump from the mainland, the privately owned, low-lying Matakana Island stretches some 20 kilometres across the seaward side of Tauranga Harbour in the western Bay of Plenty. Pigs are low in number here according to Dave Bragg, the district manager of a large commercial exotic forest on the island. Within the forest an open season is held from May to August, partly because of the fire season, and partly to conserve the sport. The local pig-hunting club is permitted to liberate a dozen or so pigs each year into the forested areas; a unique situation that might, eventually, become commonplace in this country.

◦ ◦ D'Urville Island

With a total area of 4090 hectares, this rugged landmass on the eastern side of Tasman Bay is by far the largest of the outer islands of the Marlborough Sounds. It consists of DoC (about one-third), Maori and privately owned land, mostly small-holdings rather than farms.

Local identity Pip Alpin told me that pigs are a lot more visible on the island than they are in other parts of the country, and that numbers were fairly high. There is some hunting by islanders, but because D'Urville Island is so hard to get to, mainlanders tend to shy away. Moreover, according to Pip, locals do not welcome pig-hunters with dogs and firearms, considering them a liability.

Peter Brady of DoC says that pigs roam the island in big mobs, rooting up vast areas of land. However, there is little to be gained by sending in a hit team because many of the landowners whose properties adjoined DoC land more or less farmed wild pigs — in such circumstances hunting DoC land would be a pointless exercise. Today D'Urville Island carries possibly the highest concentration of feral pigs in the country. They could be classed as a pig of medium size, running from black to assorted colours.

◦ ◦ Arapawa Island

Pigs found on this large island in the Marlborough Sounds are mostly of average size and, while varied in colour, they are generally black. The numbers are considered higher than the national average, the reason being lack of hunting pressure. DoC has an agreement with local landowners not to issue hunting permits for its reserve without prior

The wild pig is both adaptable and resourceful.

Puketi Forest is typical of many exotic and native forests in Northland where pigs can be found.

Arapawa Island is one of several offshore islands where pigs are well established.

At Preservation Inlet (a part of Coal Island), in Fiordland National Park, the pigs are seldom disturbed by hunters.

The Longwood Range in Southland, where forest, scrub and pastureland merge together, could be classed as perfect pig habitat.

Pigs will eat anything, including (from left) the roots of snow tussock, a rabbit, and the roots of Spaniard grass.

Sweet briar.

consent to cross private land, so the number of hunting permits issued is very small.

◦ ◦ Blumine Island

To my knowledge, there had only been one 'illegal' liberation of pigs on an offshore island during the 1980s. The island is Blumine, and it is located in Queen Charlotte Sound, on the western side of Arapawa Island.

There have been pigs on Blumine for many years; a Lands and Survey file from 1917 refers to the island by its commonly used name: Pig Island. In more recent times, old pig sign was reported on the island in 1957 by an NZDA hunting party, and in 1961 members of the Forest and Bird Protection Society found pig sign to be common. In the same year, a Wildlife Service party came across pig sign, and more was found in 1970. Eleven years later, a botanical party did not find any sign of pigs. Four years later, however, a DoC scientist, studying *Powelliphanta* snails, did see evidence of pigs; they were a major cause of this unique species's decline on the mainland. A liberation, then, was made some time between 1983 and 1987.

A DoC hunting team, using dogs, went to Blumine in 1988 and 1989. They eliminated a number of pigs, including a barrow.

◦ ◦ Chatham Islands

This far-flung, three-strong cluster of islands in the South Pacific is about 700 kilometres south-east of Wellington. The largest island in the group is Chatham, with a total area of 90,000 hectares; next in size is Pitt, being 6190 hectares, and last of all, South-East Island, a mere 260 hectares. On Chatham and Pitt, pigs are fairly common, but there are none on South-East. The government owns very little land here, about eight percent, which includes a number of small islets. Pigs are light on the ground on DoC land, and unless they are causing trouble, any control is left in the hands of a private hunter force, which might number ten hardy souls using dogs.

Generally speaking, the habitat on the main Chatham Island suits pigs very well. Much of the original forest has long since gone and fern and nikau have taken control, along with rank grass, blackberry bushes, and so on. The pigs are similar in both size and temperament to those on the mainland; lamb-killers are not uncommon. Black is the most regularly seen colour here.

◦ ◦ Auckland Islands

In December 1989 the Department of Conservation sent a team to the Auckland Islands, to, among other things, find out if the Auckland Island rail was still alive (it hadn't been observed for about 30 years), study the yellow-eyed penguin, and continue the Department's wild goat eradication policy. At this time pigs were found only on the main Auckland Island, and the two hunters accounted for twenty of them. Wild pigs had almost eliminated *Pleurophyllum, Stilbocarpa* and *Anisotome* from the island, except in the steepest country. They had nearly wiped out the ground-burrowing prions and petrels, and also fed on yellow-eyed penguins and shags.

An estimated 1000 pigs range the 40,600-hectare island and, although they are often found in the alpine regions, which this far south is anything above 170 metres, they tend to favour the coastal areas. They like to forage on the beaches, feeding on seaweed or whatever is washed up — even dead whales. The sows here tend to have smaller litters than those on the mainland, and the pigs are a good size, running up to around the 200-pound live weight mark for top boars. They are multi-coloured, with black predominating.

By 1992, goats were all but wiped out on all the Auckland Islands, but to rid the main island of pigs would be a long-term project, and an ambitious one. It may well be that DoC will leave things pretty much as they are for a while and then assess the situation.

To bring this particular chapter to a close, please allow me to indulge myself a little . . .

In the mid 1970s a lighthouse keeper decided to take a very young pig with him to Stephens Island, three kilometres off the northern end of D'Urville Island. The idea was that he would fatten it up as a special treat for Christmas.

So by launch to Stephens Island went one little pig. There are no landing places on the island; the cliffs are very nearly perpendicular. Therefore it is a tricky and dangerous job to bring the launch in below the towering cliffs and to hold it there while a large box is lowered from above by a powerful winch. Once on deck, the box is loaded with supplies, and sometimes people, and hauled up. Meantime, the captain of the launch, because of the roughness of the sea, must circle away, to move back in again while the whole process is repeated. By this time-consuming method, then, one little pig, no doubt totally bemused, arrived on Stephens Island.

Naturally enough, the pig ended up in a sty and the lighthouse keeper, one of several manning the light at that time, went on with the unending business of looking after the most powerful lighthouse in the country, visible for at least 50 kilometres. He and his family lived in one of several small cottages; this was the extent of human impact on the island.

At first, the pig sorely missed his family: his mother, his brothers and his sisters. Later, as Christmas approached, he sensed there was an ominous reason why he was cooped up. He yearned to be free, not trapped, forced to survive on slops, standing in his own excrement, perhaps dying a little day by day.

The pig naturally did what so many other pigs in captivity have done.

He seized the day and escaped, fast, free-ranging, a prisoner no longer. To fend for itself. The pig's new home was a sharp-backed ridge rearing out of the sea. It was some 2000 metres long by around 1400 metres wide, the highest point was 283 metres. The slopes were mostly tussock-clad, and there was a belt of typically stunted Cook Strait forest comprising kohekohe, kawakawa, mahoe, supplejack and the occasional nikau palm working hard to simply exist in such a wind-blasted environment.

A pig, of course, could survive here by rooting up tussock, poking industriously around the forest. Finding food was never going to be a problem. The island is a wildlife sanctuary, the habitat of the tuatara, the unique Stephens Island frog and countless sea-birds, most notably fairy prions. At the time of the pig's escape the fairy prions were nesting on the island, where they are estimated to number one million. They nest in huge, incredibly noisy colonies.

Learning of the pig's escape, the lighthouse keeper was both furious and more than a little embarrassed. After all, what he had done was illegal; there was no way anyone would be granted official permission to bring a pig onto Stephens Island. Mistakes, he reasoned, could be rectified without anyone being any the wiser. He would seek out the pig. With luck there would still be roast pork on the table come Christmas.

Time after time the lighthouse keeper hunted the elusive pig. Christmas came and went and he had not found a single trace of the pig. He believed the pig had died, not knowing how to survive in the wild. So he put his rifle to one side; the matter was best forgotten.

The pig had known to stay out of sight of the lighthouse keeper. He remembered the man's smell, associating it with the sty, captivity and all that implied. No more of that! Also, the powerful inner forces that motivated him were already at work, making him react differently to the way he had in the sty, making him behave like a hunted animal.

The pig had found himself in a gigantic supermarket where he was the single shopper. He simply went from one burrow to the next, devouring the white eggs or down-coated chicks of the grey-blue petrels. He may also have partaken of the leathery eggs and young of the tuatara, for they often nest in the same burrows as the petrels. Apart from eating the odd hatchling, the tuatara has a fairly harmonious relationship with the petrel.

Well into the new year the pig, perhaps a little incautious, happened to wander closer to the lighthouse. He was spotted. The lighthouse keeper, shocked to hear the pig was still alive, grabbed his rifle, but it was too late — the pig was gone.

Once more the hunt for the only pig to set foot on Stephens Island began, but again the lighthouse keeper was unable to find the pig. There was, he knew, only one thing to do: contact the proper authorities and hope they would take a lenient view of his foolish action. The matter ended up in the hands of the Wildlife Service. Fortunately they did not take the matter too seriously and reasoned that one young pig should pose few problems for an expert pig-hunter operating with dogs on a comparatively small island. The hunter duly accounted for the pig, which, if only for a few short months, had gone wild. He found it where petrels were nesting — he had never seen a fatter pig in his entire life!

A Matter of Anonymity

It was 1977, and winter was closing fast on spring. A rather battered Land-Rover barrelled along State Highway 6 a few kilometres north of Cromwell; the headlights stabbed a dazzling pathway through the deceptive light of the pre-dawn. It was frosty, and the driver, fearful that black ice would send him skidding off the road, drove with caution.

On his left he could see a dark, almost ominous, landmass against the ever-lightening sky; this was the Pisa Range, rearing up between the valleys of the Cardrona River to the west and the Clutha River to the east. Mount Pisa, the highest point on the range at 1961 metres, was named by the Otago surveyor John Turnbull Thomson, who thought that one of its rocky outcrops looked like the famous 'leaning tower'. The driver pressed on, lost in thought. Like Thomson he was about to make history.

By 1977 it was rare to see red deer on the Pisa Range, a far cry from the days before helicopter hunting, when stationmen shot them for dog tucker and trophy hunters in search of a 'royal' 40 x 40 inch head were often in luck. Chamois had also fallen victim to the chopper boys, but, since they were never in high demand overseas, they had not suffered to the same extent. Now they could be found on the range in small, well-scattered family groups.

Wild pigs on the Pisa Range? Why not? It was likely pig habitat. The lower slopes on the eastern, western and southern aspects of the range were largely unbroken, a riot of manuka, fern, bracken, blackberry and, perhaps most significantly, sweet briar. Yet by the late winter of 1977, no wild pig had ever set foot on the Pisa Range.

Presently, the driver observed to his left the gateway to Mount Pisa station. His destination was close now; a secretive smile stole across his unshaven features. Beyond Mount Pisa lay another fine run: Lochaburn. On reaching its southern boundary, the driver started to slow down. The headlights picked up a closed, but not locked, iron gate on the left side of the road. The driver dipped the headlights and applied the brake.

The unsealed road was dusty and badly corrugated and the driver, his work-hardened hands clamped like limpets to rock around the steering wheel felt suddenly uneasy. Ahead, now, lay Lochaburn Gully. He somehow forced himself to relax. He knew this big country well, had hunted it often for red deer in the 'good old days'.

The potholes in the road became increasingly common and the Land-Rover, past its best, rattled and groaned. To the east, directly behind the driver, lay the Dunstan Mountains, an impressive backdrop to both Bendigo and Northburn stations. A candy-floss flush, growing tenfold by the second, appeared about the raggedy-ridged peaks. Moments later the sun, a big red ball, an almost tangible god, began to lift itself above the mountains and a sudden burst of light extended across the Clutha Valley and exploded upon the tops of the Pisa Range.

The driver's eyes lifted from the road; the range, its tussock crest gleaming, appeared to be directly above him, but ahead of him in the dark lay ridge upon ridge, fold upon fold of foothills country. Soon the driver stopped: this was as good a place as any. He switched off the ignition and the engine died with a throaty rasping sound. He clambered outside. Cold, all right, a light breeze with teeth in it, blowing from the south, invariably a sign of fine weather. He rubbed his hands together briskly, then stopped and listened with his head cocked to one side like a kea perched on a mountain beech tree. Nothing. He chuckled softly. He had deliberately chosen a Sunday morning, when the stationmen would be having a welcome lie-in.

The tall, somewhat round-shouldered man in his late thirties spun on his heel and went to the back of the Land-Rover. He took hold of the dust-coated tailgate and gave it a hard yank. It opened reluctantly, then the stench of fresh excrement assailed him. He reached in and took hold of the nearest wriggling sack. Without apparent effort, for he was surprisingly strong, the man carted the sack, its contents bunched awkwardly against his chest, a short distance and then without ceremony dumped it on the ground. He repeated the process until only one sack remained in the Land-Rover. He paused then and breathed deeply; his heart, he realised, was hammering.

Again he listened: a faint breeze rather than a light wind moved through the nearby scrub. Quickly, he carried the last sack and its heavy load — about 90 pounds, he reckoned — to join the others. Kneeling, he fished about in a jacket pocket and produced a folding knife. With a deft movement, he cut through the green twine around the neck of one of the sacks, pulled back the coarse material, and a moment later a head appeared. The man stepped back as with snakelike movements a young pig — a sow — materialised from the sacking. She stood there, bewildered.

Now the man opened three more sacks, each of which contained another young sow. The sows were all pregnant for the first time, perhaps six to eight months old. Each was reddish-brown, a shade difficult to pinpoint, say, in a patch of snow tussock. They were typical of pigs that since the late 1970s had gradually infiltrated Central Otago from the east through Danseys Pass.

The man turned his attention to the last sack; it obviously held a much bigger animal. From it emerged a coal-black boar, blinking as though it had just awoken after a long sleep on a sun-warmed grassy slope. A misconception, of course; the boar was fully awake and potentially dangerous. Wisely, the man stepped well away. Like the sows, the boar had been held captive for several weeks and drenched for worms and ticks. The man believed in doing a job right.

Meantime, the sows had retreated to a patch of cover. Typical of their species, they were conversing freely. The boar homed in on the sows with a fast, tail-swinging gait. He had the look of a Te Anau pig about him.

The man smiled; all had gone well. With luck it would be some time before anyone around here knew they had pigs on the range. By then they would have multiplied dramatically. At any rate, there was nothing else he could do. It was in the lap of the gods. Nevertheless, he had a powerful hunch that they would make out, pigs being what they were. With that thought, the man gathered the foul-smelling sacks and dumped them in the back of the Land-Rover. Then with the near-blinding rays of the sun shafting across the valley bottom, he headed out to the main road.

In effect, then, this was the first liberation of wild pigs on the Pisa Range. The reason? I suppose we could say it was for nothing more than sporting purposes, yet there was also some degree of devilment in there, too. It was of course nothing new in rural New Zealand. Since the very early days both Maori and Pakeha have been doing exactly the same thing.

Three or four months later he and two similarly minded accomplices would return at night to Lochaburn station to liberate a further four pigs — three Central Otago sows and a young greyish boar from South Canterbury. The idea was to release pigs of mixed blood and thus prevent in-breeding. The following year, the roguish trio turned their attention to Waitere station, at the southern end of the Pisa Range. Four pigs were set free off State Highway 6 as it swept through the rugged Kawarau Gorge by Roaring Meg Stream. The country up in there was steep with many gullies and much heavy cover. Ideal pig habitat.

Later still our original rogue turned his attention to Mount Burke and its sister run, Glen Dene, in an attempt to establish pigs throughout the region. Twenty pigs were involved in three liberations; this, coupled with the fact that pigs were already working their way here under their own steam, would ensure that there would always be good pig-hunting in the area. Next in line was Minaret station, across Lake Wanaka from The Neck. In broad daylight, the pigs were taken across the lake in a powerful launch and set free in a little bay no distance from the homestead. There would be a second liberation on Minaret by different people soon after, a total of about a dozen pigs all up. Pigs would also turn up on West Wanaka and Cattle Flat station.

Here on the sun-warmed Pisa Range, where the year-round climate could be judged temperate, the pigs could root away to their hearts' content with their flexible, leathery snouts, uncovering edible sustenance below ground level amidst the fern, bracken or pastureland, or up higher, around the 1000-metre mark, where big snow tussocks and Spaniard grass flourished.

In Europe the industrious digging and rooting of a wild boar is considered useful, as it stimulates forest growth by turning over the earth and allowing it to aerate. By and large this results in conditions that favour the germination and development of new plants. The same thing has naturally happened in the numerous indigenous and exotic forests in this country, but local woodsmen and foresters have always looked upon such rooting antics unfavourably.

Depending on the season, there were many foods a Pisa Range pig could eat other than, for example, the starch-rich, carrot-like roots of Spaniard grass. In summer the small gooseberry bushes were overloaded with ripe fruit, yellowing in the sun, and in winter there was sweet briar. There was no shortage of sweet briar: entire hillfaces were covered with the tenacious growth, a mass of vivid scarlet. The brilliant red berries, from which rosehip syrup is made, contain a powerful dose of vitamin C. We may presume there were few pigs with runny noses on the Pisa Range during winter.

The introduced sweet briar was first offered for sale by nurserymen in Christchurch as far back as 1861. Like another importation, broom, its introduction to the high-country runs of the South Island was a disaster. By 1900 sweet briar, along with blackberry and the Californian thistle, was classified as a noxious weed.

In 1948, Bill Chisholm was the manager of the government-owned Molesworth station. Located on the Marlborough–Canterbury border, it was by far the biggest pastoral run in the country. The knew all about sweet briar there, and knew heaps about pigs, too. In a letter Bill Chisholm wrote to George Martin, the Commissioner of Lands in Blenheim, he spelled out on the effects of sweet briar.

> Sweet brier is strongly competing with the rabbit for the total destruction of some of our back country grazing areas in the South Island. The spread on Molesworth has been rather alarming but the Department should in no way feel apologetic for its introduction and spread. Neighbouring properties in this locality are equally infested: Upcot, Middlehurst, Langridge, Muller, Bluff, Clarence Reserve, St Helens and Molesworth-Tarndale each have vast areas involved. These neighbouring properties are grazed by sheep and although the spread on them is more rapid than that on Molesworth, nevertheless

brier is increasing on them.

Grazing animals (pigs, horses, cattle, deer, goats) are responsible for the spread, in particular the pig, which has been the largest contributing cause on Molesworth. In the Elliot, where brier is worst, pigs have been very numerous. Some 2000 were shot to try and combat the spread of brier; this resulted in a noticeable increase in rabbits on which they also feed.

As a matter of interest, a study of a particularly obliging wild boar over a period of several weeks revealed some rather peculiar feeding habits. The boar stalked rabbits to the exclusion of all other animals. He was a smart boar, too. Reaching a warren, he systematically blocked off all possible exits except one. Then, displaying unusual strength and ingenuity, he began to dig down into the last remaining hole and was able to trap one unfortunate rabbit after another in the side galleries or chambers.

We can assume with confidence that there were pigs on the Pisa Range that were partial to rabbits and hares, providing they could catch this long-legged speedster. Other foods would have included chunky, protein-rich morsels like rats or smaller titbits such as country mice and various insects.

The wild pig is among the world's great scavengers, up there with the hyena, saltwater crocodile, dingo and ostrich. The pig is equipped with a marvellous sense of smell and from a great distance this sense can guide him unerringly to all sorts of culinary delights. On the Pisa Range that could include the carrion of stock, goats, hedgehogs, rabbits, hares, birds, whatever. Like a saltwater crocodile, a pig prefers this sort of meal to be well matured, the more rotten and maggot-ridden the better.

The Forest Service Steps In

The problem of wild pigs on the Pisa Range ended up in 1982 on the already overloaded desk of District Ranger Roly Martin, at Forest Service headquarters, Queenstown. A tanned, burly type, Martin had been with the Department since the mid 1960s. He had started out as a track cutter and rung by slippery rung had gradually worked his way up the bureaucratic ladder. A caring and compassionate man, with a deep understanding of wildlife in general, Martin held unorthodox views about conserving wild animals — in particular fallow deer in the famed Greenstone/Caples area — that would bring him into conflict with his 1950s-thinking superiors, who, to be blunt, still believed that the only good deer was a dead deer.

The dilemma posed by wild pigs on the Pisa Range was the least of Martin's problems. Over the last four or five years, there had been a steady build-up in their numbers throughout Central Otago. Martin considered it essential to conduct a survey of pig numbers on the Pisa Range, to allow him to determine what action to take. But first he would visit some of the runholders who had voiced their concern; later, he intended to call on various people in the Tarras/Hawea area, including one man in particular . . .

In the third week of May 1982, Martin, accompanied by Forest Service Ranger Colin McKinney, visited the stations that backed on to the Pisa Range: Low Burn, Mount Pisa, Lochaburn, Queensberry Ridges, Criffel, Larches, Mid Run, Cliffburn, Waiorau and Avalon. There were pigs on all of these runs and the general opinion of all but Criffel station, where they favoured control by station staff and their friends, was that the Forest Service should take positive action.

There were no objections when Martin requested that a survey of pig numbers be carried out on their land. Sensible, of course. In 1982 the Forest Service still carried a big stick and, if required, knew only too well how to use it. One morning at the end of June Rangers Martin and McKinney visited the Tarras/Hawea region. They arrived at the residence of the man they believed to have first liberated pigs on the Pisa Range, and, if pub talk was to be believed, in other areas, too. The man was not at home. For lack of hard evidence, no charges were ever brought against anyone connected with these pig liberations, even though it is common knowledge in Central Otago precisely who they are.

Next, the rangers went to see Hec Wilson, the recently retired supervisor of the Lindis/Hawea Pest Destruction Board. Had pigs been recently sighted in the areas he was familiar with? Sure they had, but it would make far more sense, Wilson continued, if they paid a call on Bill Johnsen, who had recently taken over his position. They thanked Hec Wilson and then found out that Johnsen was expected home for lunch.

With time to spare, they visited Gerald Goodyear, a deerculler in the days of the Internal Affairs Department, who now farmed in the area. Goodyear told them that he and the other farmers in the district were alarmed at the steady increase in pig numbers and the fact they were turning up in places that until recently had been completely free of them. Unless drastic action was taken soon, Goodyear stressed, they could expect pastures to be destroyed, and lambs to be killed.

As expected, Bill Johnsen arrived home for his midday meal. Pigs were becoming more numerous, all right, according to Johnsen. His blokes often reported seeing them; one man, he added, had seen a mob of perhaps twenty. Among the stations he listed where they had seen pigs, or their sign, was Breast Hill, roughly midway between Tarras and Omarama, west of State Highway 8.

Martin was deeply concerned to hear that pigs had been sighted on Breast Hill, specifically on the true left of Breast Creek. As far as he knew, they had never been seen there before. Of course they could have made their own way there from the St Bathans Range via Lindis Pass country, crossing State Highway 8 somewhere between Breast Hill and Morven Hills stations. But they may have been yet another cursed liberation, someone letting them go off the road.

Either way, Martin thought as they left Johnsen to finish his lunch, they had to be checked. If not, they would undoubtedly spread west, into areas of state forest, including the Dingle River and Timaru Creek. From there, given time, it would be a natural progression to the Hunter and Ahuriri Rivers. Reaching Cromwell, Martin and McKinney headed towards Wanaka rather than Queenstown, with the intention of having a few words with Reg Brown of Lochaburn station about the forthcoming pig survey.

During the course of their conservation, Brown told them that only last weekend a party of shooters after California quail had spotted a mob of pigs — at least twenty — that were upwind and completely unaware of them. The shooting party, obviously prepared for the possibility that they might run into pigs, had time to break open their guns and replace their lightly loaded birdshot cartridges with potent buckshot slugs. Then they moved closer and closer until the range was short and, like a well-drilled SWAT team, they cut loose. The result was six fewer pigs in the sweet briar on Lochaburn, and a whole heap of shell-shocked live ones running around would, in future, be that much more cautious.

The Forest Service survey on the Pisa Range took place over nineteen days in July 1982. All Department staff in the Southern Lakes District were involved — a total of eleven men. The cost, including wages, food and transport, came to around $8200 of taxpayers' money. Because of the size of the area to be covered, it was decided to split the men into two teams. One party would cover the eastern side of the range, the other the western side. Using four-wheel-drives the men were taken to the start of their beats, the last one dropped off at the snow line. The driver then returned to the lowlands and, in a musterer's terms, the bottom beat. At the end of the day, he would pick up the men. Each man was, of course, armed, so it was a field survey with search-and-destroy overtones.

They covered the warm, sunny faces between 700 metres and 800 metres, above the fog belt and below the snow line. The ground was, generally speaking, on the steep side, riddled with gullies, often rocky — likely chamois habitat. It was where station staff and private hunters had reported seeing the greatest concentrations of pigs at this time of the year.

By the end of the survey they had seen fifty-one pigs. Of this number, twenty-seven fell victim to the government hot shots, mostly using .222s. As many as 80 percent of the pigs sighted were piglets or half to three-quarters grown — young stuff, not too clued up about survival. Of those shot, three were pregnant sows, due — it was judged following an autopsy — to give birth very soon. Collectively, they would have given birth to twenty-seven young.

All the evidence pointed to a small but well-established population, still in the colonisation process. Their presence was starting to tell: rooting on pastures was noticed, as well as damage to water races. Some of the pigs had a taste for carcasses, and runholders were concerned they might kill and eat lambs at birth; this had been a problem in other pig-infested areas. If the pig population increased, Martin felt, crops would be in danger. Pigs love spuds — they will travel long distances to feed on them, and what they can do to a potato crop in a night is incredible.

In short, if the population increased, it would have a serious effect on financial returns of the farms and runs in the area. Martin recommended that recreational pig-hunting be encouraged in order to maintain or lower the present populations. If this did not prove effective, or if bovine TB became a problem, further steps could be taken.

During the survey the names of three keen pig-hunters had kept cropping up as possible suspects for pig liberations. Later, Roly Martin was to discover from local talk that the suspicion was justified. There was talk of imminent liberations ranging from Kawarau River to the West Coast, so

Martin and McKinney invited two of the suspects to the Cromwell police station, where a firm discussion took place in front of a police constable. The Wild Animal Control Act was spelled out to them, as well as the consequences if they were caught. They also highlighted the problem of TB spread and the concerns of the farmers and runholders. The message was well digested.

The hunters had certainly achieved their objective on the Pisa Range. It was now up to the farmers and runholders to decide whether to allow them access.

Next in Line

Mount Burke station is in mountainous country between Lake Wanaka and Lake Hawea. The most pleasing aspects of the run, lovely sun-warmed faces, are found on the western side of the property, overlooking Lake Wanaka. The station has been in the Burdon family since 1928 and its original spread of 20,000 hectares was divided up by George Burdon's sons, Cotty and Jerry, in 1979. Cotty retained the southern section, which included the gracious old homestead near Lake Wanaka, while Jerry settled for the northern, slightly smaller, part now named Glen Dene. The Glen Dene homestead is a few kilometres north of Hawea township on State Highway 6, on a bench-like flat with a commanding view of the lake.

This is attractive country, which rises to 1417 metres at Mount Burke itself. Red deer have long found it agreeable terrain and before the advent of the helicopters they ranged the run in their thousands. Nowadays their numbers are low. The days of top trophies seem to have vanished for all time; the same, of course, can be said for much of the country, including the Pisa Range. Again as on the Pisa Range, chamois can be found on the station, in numbers compatible with the environment; they are hunted for strictly recreational purposes.

Significantly, Mount Burke station is the only place Bennett's or red-necked wallabies are found in New Zealand outside their well-established range in the Hunters Hills of South Canterbury. Their numbers, never high, don't cause concern.

On the last Sunday in June 1982 Forest Service Headman/Hunter John Fleming was enjoying a day off duty when the telephone rang. An irate Cotty Burdon was on the other end of the line with distressing news: pig rooting had been found in the Long Gully paddocks, on the eastern side of the run, facing Lake Hawea.

Fleming digested that. The last time pigs had been spotted in the area was four or five years ago. Obviously there had been a liberation. He wondered if it was the same person who'd let pigs go on Cattle Flat station.

'Much rooting?' Fleming asked.

'Too bloody much!' was the angry reply.

'More than one pig, y'reckon?'

'Looks that way.'

Both men fell silent, each churning over similar thoughts: if pigs were to ever get out of control on the place they might prove impossible to eradicate. What could provide more suitable habitat than the Pisa Range?

Finally, Cotty Burdon sighed and stated the obvious: 'So someone's gone and done the dirty on us, eh?'

Fleming's mind raced pell-mell: they had covered all of both Mount Burke and Glen Dene less than two years ago while conducting a survey on wallabies. There was no sign of pigs then.

After an even longer pause, Burdon said, 'Why in God's name would anyone want to do this to us . . .?'

As though he were facing Cotty Burdon, Fleming shrugged. Burdon's question was fair enough, but the answer was obvious: for sporting purposes, with no real thought of the long-term consequences. Cotty Burdon and the other runholders on the Pisa Range had every reason to be upset.

'John?'

'Uh-huh.'

'Listen . . . I'm hoping you boys can sort it out for me.'

Ranger Paul Hondelink's reaction to news of yet another pig liberation in his patch was exactly what Fleming expected. Fair enough. They had enough to contend with on Mount Pisa without more feral pigs being added to the hit list.

'Better check it out in the morning, John,' Hondelink said, 'and then we'll decide what to do.'

'You're hoping it isn't really pigs, right?'

Hondelink smiled without humour. 'We couldn't be that lucky, could we . . .?'

The next morning John Fleming swung his compact, muscular frame into the cabin of a Department Toyota. His dog, Mac, grinning as though he'd just heard a great joke, sat in the back. An hour later Fleming, hands on hips, stood staring at half an acre of upturned earth. With the toe of his boot, he turned over a dropping. No mistake on Cotty Burdon's part, he realised, but he really hadn't expected that. With a rueful shake of his head, he called Mac and turned on his heel.

Wanaka-raised, John Fleming had made his first big hunting trips on Cattle Flat station, up the Matukituki River, with his father, Jack, and Ivan Carson, in the mid 1950s. Carson was employed on the local Rabbit Board and had been one of Captain Franklyn ('the skipper') Yerex's initial band of Internal Affairs Department hunters when in 1930 the government, under intense pressure from high-country runholders, had finally declared deer and other wild animals such as thar and chamois to be pests. Carson and his contemporaries became known, rather inaccurately, as the deercullers.

In light of what later happened on Mount Burke station, it was significant that, quite apart from the inevitable red deer, there were also pigs on Cattle Flat station. They were there for a reason — to control vast areas of fern — and the first release of a big Tamworth boar and several sows had taken place as far back as the early 1930s. Dave Aubrey, who owned the run, would make two more liberations, the last in the early 1940s. Aubrey genuinely liked pigs and the word in the Wanaka district was you could forget all about shooting pigs on Cattle Flat station. Over the years the pigs gradually increased in numbers in a smallish area around Niger Creek. Naturally enough, the odd pig wandered onto the adjoining run, Mount Aspiring station, where Jerry Aspinall's orders were direct: pigs were to be shot on sight!

By the time John Fleming and his older companions turned up on Cattle Flat station the wild pigs numbered in the thousands. Driving in to the station it was not unusual to have several hundred bolting across the road in front of you, or to look to the ferny hillfaces and observe mobs thirty-strong on rooting duty. Cattle Flat station would have been a pig-hunter's paradise — if pig-hunting was allowed.

Nothing, however, lasts forever. When Dave Aubrey died, his son, Rod, took control of Cattle Flat station. Rod, unlike his rather sentimental father, considered the pigs weren't controlling fern as effectively as they might. Furthermore, the ever-increasing numbers were turning their attention to grassy paddocks rather than unproductive fern hillfaces. That would never do; the pigs were removed from the protected list.

The word flashed around the Wanaka country: on Cattle Flat station pigs were an open go! And go for it many keen boys did — some of them, even without dogs, were taking up to sixty animals a day. If that wasn't enough, the Forest Service, having taken over the responsibility of wild animal control from the Internal Affairs Department in 1956, sent two contract shooters, George and Frank Erceg, to Cattle Flat. The brothers, top guns in any company, did not miss too many pigs with their open-sighted .303s. Towards the end of the 1960s pigs were there in low, well-scattered numbers, ranging mostly open country, easy targets for the chopper boys on venison recovery operations. By 1970 feral pigs on Cattle Flat station were definitely endangered.

Meantime, in 1960, John Fleming, fired by Ivan Carson's stirring tales of huge tallies, remote camps, great mates, and everything else that was part and parcel of a deerculling life, had taken the plunge and joined the Forest Service. He, too, became a government hunter; a way of life that suited him perfectly. But like many a deerculler in the mid to late 1960s, Fleming quit his job, tempted away by the big money that could be made shooting for meat.

In appearance there is very little difference between this feral pig and the true wild boar from which it originated. This particular boar could weigh 300 pounds on the hoof.

Pigs are frequently found in pine plantations, from which they emerge to forage, usually at night.

The sow is a dedicated, caring mother who will, in response to her young's call of distress, come running with great urgency.

Time for a drink. The fact that the water is muddy does not matter in the least: soil contains essential iron.

While a pig has a wonderful sense of smell and acute hearing, its eyesight is poor, which explains why this pig is unsure of the photographer.

This brownish piglet, striped of coat, is a dead ringer for the young of the true wild boar.

Pig rooting scars a hillface on a Southland farm. Wild pigs are notorious for destroying large areas of good pastureland by digging down a metre or more to find food.

In the early morning, and almost caught in the act of rooting, a medium-sized boar is moments away from moving to cover.

A favourite haunt of his to hunt red deer was, naturally enough, Cattle Flat station. One day while heading in to the station, he came to the Niger Creek. Here was the biggest patch of manuka and scrub left on the run; the place where years ago there had been so many pigs. Driving slowly — for you were likely to see a deer anywhere — he suddenly spotted a big, dark shape up in the fern. Braking, he recognised it for a pig, the first he had seen there in quite some time. Since you could sell the carcass of a pig as easily as that of a deer, although it wasn't worth as much per pound, Fleming grabbed his rifle and went after the unsuspecting animal.

The huge black sow with a grey fleck running through her stiff-haired coat was moving slowly along. All that ended when a .243 projectile, fired from a Browning semi-automatic rifle, caught up with her. Dressed out, the sow would weigh close to 300 pounds; sows, Fleming knew, did not come much bigger. This particular animal proved to be the last remaining link on Cattle Flat station with the untold numbers of feral pigs that had lived and died there in a span of nearly forty years. It would be about ten years — the early 1980s — before pigs again turned up in the area of Niger Creek on Cattle Flat station.

By this time, John Fleming was back on the Forest Service payroll as a headman/hunter based in Hawea, answering to Ranger Paul Hondelink. When word came down the line from Cattle Flat station that pig rooting had been observed in Niger Creek, Hondelink wasted little time in sending out his number-one trouble shooter to deal with the problem. Fleming took with him a curly-coated retriever called Mac. This was a top-notch hunting dog that indicated the presence of game — deer or goats — by pointing. He had no experience with pigs, however.

Precisely who had liberated pigs on Cattle Flat station is unclear. What is certain, however, is that the boar was a good size, in excess of 200 pounds, and was slate-grey in colour, indicating a possible connection with Canterbury. The sow was small and brownish with a few dark spots, most likely a local animal: from Central Otago or more towards the eastern coastline. They had produced six multicoloured youngsters by the time John Fleming and an eager Mac arrived on the scene.

Fleming parked his vehicle some distance from the rooting and started on foot towards it. Mac, silent as a puff of smoke, trailed behind. The pigs were out in the open, rooting on the river flats, the young ones doing a fair job of emulating their industrious parents. Fleming checked his BSA Majestic .222. Good. With the wind in his favour and Mac behaving himself, he moved in. Close enough to hear the pigs babbling amongst themselves. With economy of movement, Fleming put the classy triple-two through its paces, dropping, in sequence, the boar, sow, and one of the now fast-departing youngsters. They were, he knew, old enough to fend for themselves; he would have to return. A few days, then, or maybe a week . . . give them time to settle down.

Meanwhile, an excited but puzzled Mac investigated the dead animals, growling like an enraged teddy bear. Little did he know how very big a part pigs were going to play in his life. The same thing could, of course, be said of his master.

A week later, Fleming returned to Cattle Flat station and eliminated four of the five remaining piglets. About a year later a musterer accounted for the sole survivor.

Now, some years later, John Fleming was returning home to Hawea after checking out the pig rooting on Mount Burke station. As the Toyota sped along the highway, Fleming's dark brown eyes roamed restlessly over the station's eastern flanks. Lovely country. Rolling hills before the mountains took control. A mass of fern, like a many-hued carpet, spread across the lower slopes. Fleming smiled; it occurred to him that whoever had liberated pigs on Mount Burke station had chosen exactly the right spot.

Next day, in the company of Paul Hondelink, he returned to the scene of Cotty Burdon's most recent dilemma. Fresh rooting — only a few hours old, Fleming judged — greeted the Forest Service men. Mac investigated the upturned earth with a mixture of excitement and curiosity. Hondelink and Fleming decided to work over a big gully that was more or less directly behind the rooting. A long day produced no result. They returned the following day; again no luck. This feral pig was proving highly elusive.

By the late afternoon of the third day both men were a little disgruntled by their lack of success. As they followed a long, leading ridge, with the last of the big gully on their left, they discussed the news they had heard yesterday: that a bulldozer driver, while working on a stock track between the two stations, but still on the Mount Burke side, had seen three pigs, including a big boar, running up a ridge. It was very hard to believe — the rooting they had seen indicated there was only one pig in the area.

Fleming decided to cut across the gully to a bulldozed track that followed a similar easterly trending ridge.

'Never know your luck, right?' Fleming said as he snapped two fingers together; Mac responded at once.

'Luck?' Hondelink briefly raised his eyes to the overcast sky. 'We could use some of that.'

Looking back over his shoulder at the tall blond man, Fleming chuckled.

'Pick you up at the gate,' Hondelink called.

'Right.' Fleming half raised a hand.

The bulldozed track twisted and coiled between low hillocks and scattered clumps of tussock. Several Hereford cattle watched Fleming with suspicion from a nearby ridge; fern brushed their bloated bellies. Out on State Highway 6 — only a few hundred metres away — a car caught Fleming's eye. All over for the day, he thought. He pulled a face: three full days without success was just not his style.

Suddenly Mac, ranging ahead, stopped, stiffened and pointed. Fleming looked for a hare or a rabbit, but instead spotted a medium-sized, chocolate-coloured pig on the track only a short distance away. It might have materialised out of thin air. A split second later the pig spun about and broke into a dead run.

The Browning cracked four times, the shots so close together that it sounded like one blast. Wounded by one of the shots, the sow, lurching like a drunken seaman ashore for the first time in months, somehow remained upright and plunged into thick cover. Mac went after it, fast. So did Fleming. The dog barked in triumph on reaching the stricken animal's side and again the Browning shattered the stillness of the evening.

By the time Fleming had dragged the sow onto the track, Hondelink, grinning from ear to ear, was clambering out of the Toyota. Elated, they both examined the dead animal, noting that her mostly chocolate-brown coat was decorated with a number of black patches. Her left ear was completely missing. Dogs?

Paul Hondelink was quite certain that the pig problem on Mount Burke was sorted. The gully was later searched and no new pig sign was found. The old droppings and rooting also matched the pig. But two weeks later fresh pig rooting was discovered on Mount Burke station and the news was received by Paul Hondelink with all the appetite of a strict vegetarian faced with a greasy pork chop for breakfast. What now of bulldozer driver Neville May's report that he had seen three pigs on Mount Burke station?

On a cold July morning only a few weeks after this latest sign of pigs had been observed, Hondelink and Fleming were on State Highway 6, heading to the Kid's Bush Picnic Area, where they intended to carry out general maintenance work. Soon they were running parallel with Glen Dene station. While Fleming drove and Mac peered with interest over his shoulder, Hondelink's blue eyes were constantly roaming. High up, near a few cabbage trees, Hondelink noticed a movement. Stock? No, he thought not. He then saw another movement — an animal of roughly the same size. It looked like chamois and he said as much to Fleming. The headman/hunter simply nodded; chamois were old news on Mount Burke and Glen Dene.

Hondelink glanced up again at the dark-looking animals. Suddenly, there were several more. A puzzled expression came to his face: since when did chamois move with short, jerky movements?

He placed a restraining hand on Fleming's arm. 'Hold on a sec, mate!'

'Huh?'

'Wanna check something out.'

Fleming pulled over to the side of the road not far from Horseshoe Bend. Grabbing his field-glasses, Hondelink sprang outside and moments later gasped, 'Shit!'

Fleming was by his side now. 'What?'

'Pigs!'

'Pigs?' Fleming echoed.

'Yeah — pigs! Here, take a look for yourself.' He thrust the 8 x 30s into

Fleming's eager hands.

For several minutes, Fleming watched the pigs foraging. He counted eight . . . nine . . . ten. 'Whole mob up there, Paul.'

'Right!' Hondelink shook his head.

If they could see so many pigs from just one point, and more sign had been observed on Mount Burke station, and the bulldozer driver had seen three pigs, then just how many were there on both stations?

'What now?' Fleming asked.

'Now we shoot back to Hawea and get our rifles.'

Perhaps forty-five minutes later the two men and Mac began to climb up towards the foraging pigs. With a stiff westerly whipping in through The Neck, they eventually reached the level where, a few minutes ago, the pigs were. Hondelink ranged ahead; he was the first to see a pig. Black and medium sized, it was working over a patch of dry cow dung — underneath it would be moist, a great place to find succulent worms or crunchy-backed beetles.

Fleming and Mac ghosted up alongside Hondelink, who gave his companion a tight-lipped smile. Then Hondelink indicated his rifle. Fleming nodded as more pigs edged into view. Together they took aim. The pigs worked with enthusiasm. Simultaneous shots rang out and two pigs went down, jack-knifing. Further shots filled the air even before the reverberating blast of the first had died. Frantically the pigs charged into dense, waist-deep fern, heading down to Stewarts Creek. A sharp command from Fleming checked Mac in mid stride.

'Two's better than one, I guess,' Hondelink said as he thumbed a fresh round into the breach of his rifle.

Fleming shrugged, non-committal. Mac didn't have anything to offer, either.

Grimly, Hondelink stared at the dead pigs, mulling over those that had escaped. Action to eliminate them had to be taken at once.

Within a matter of weeks, a foot survey to ascertain pig range on Mount Burke and Glen Dene stations was carried out. Pigs were inhabiting many catchments, particularly where cover was dense. The pigs had been living where very little human activity took place; that was why no one had known of their existence — well, almost no one. In fact, it was around eighteen months after they had been liberated on Mount Burke station that it was understood that a serious problem existed.

Over the next year, and throughout 1983, the Forest Service carried out regular pig surveys on both stations; Mac's ability to find and bail pigs gained momentum with every mission. Close contact was maintained with station staff and any fresh evidence of pigs, either actual sightings or sign, was quickly relayed to Paul Hondelink or John Fleming. By the end of 1983, bearing in mind that Paul Hondelink and John Fleming had more than enough to cope with without wild pigs, they killed a total of thirty pigs in the area. A further twenty-two pigs were killed by August 1984.

No Real End to It

Meantime, there had been several reports received by the Forest Service of pigs sighted by motorists around the Lindis Pass; some, in fact, had been observed crossing State Highway 8 and heading west towards Breast Creek. This, coupled with the information Roly Martin had, prompted Paul Hondelink and his .222-toting sidekick, John Fleming, to find out at first hand what the story was.

They found some pig rooting in a small area by Breast Creek; it appeared to be made by two or three pigs and didn't warrant any action other than yearly inspection. However, pressure of work meant that the follow-up survey of wild pigs on the Pisa Range wasn't carried out until winter 1984.

A team led by Bryne Barron circumnavigated the whole of the Pisa Range, giving extra attention to known pig areas. Most of the survey was in the lower areas of the range: snow restricted movement in the upper altitudes. Each man took a beat from the snow line down a prominent ridge, and walked through on a rough contour line.

In some areas there were isolated patches of pig sign, but, although this sign was fresh, no pigs were sighted. Other areas where pig sign had been found in the first survey were now clear. The bulk of the pig sign was found around Sheepskin Creek and Fallburn; in this area fifteen pigs were sighted, of which four were confirmed kills.

Bryne Barron was able to write an optimistic report: pig numbers had reduced drastically, there was less fresh sign, and the extent of pig-affected country had decreased. However, Barron remarked on the high level of possum sign and suggested that control, possibly by commercial skin hunters, might be necessary.

Six weeks later, in August 1984, Ian Sarginson of the Dingleburn station was flying his fixed-wing aircraft to the north of the mouth of the Dingleburn River when, to his surprise, he spotted a large pig. Banking around, the better to see it, he saw a black-and-tan animal making tracks in a northerly direction, further up the lower Hunter Valley. Sarginson's surprise was understandable: no pig had ever been seen in the Hunter Valley before! He wasted little time in contacting the Forest Service's man in Hawea.

Paul Hondelink inspected the area and, although no pigs were sighted, some tracking and pig rooting were seen. The tracking indicated at least two pigs that had not been in the area very long. Was this another deliberate liberation? This was a strong possibility, but they could have arrived under their own steam from the Breast Creek country or the Ahuriri River valley. More likely the first.

A month later, a party of private hunters went to Green Bush hut on the same station. On the vehicle track south of the hut they sighted a single pig. Later, still on the true left of the Hunter River, Frank Woolf, a possum trapper who had shot over 2000 red deer as a government shooter in the Hunter in the 1955 season, came across pig rooting above Green Bush Gully. Later still, on two separate occasions, helicopter pilot Alan Duncan saw a lone pig opposite Scrubby hut, midway up the same valley and again on the true left. Shortly after this, stationmen discovered pig rooting on a spur between the lower Dingle River and Timaru Creek. By early 1986, mobs of pigs were being seen frequently near, and south of, Timaru Creek.

In February 1985, the Forest Service took another close look at the Pisa Range and was able to conclude that small numbers of pigs were well established throughout the Pisa Range. Any pig activity was being keenly followed up by runholders, with the pigs shot — or chased onto adjoining properties!

It was the late summer of 1985. Clad in his habitual shorts, Ranger Paul Hondelink, all 1.96 metres of him, strode towards the Hawea post office cum general store to pick up the mail and a few groceries. Lost in thought, Hondelink came to a sudden stop, his widening blue eyes drawn like a magnet to the occupants of a small cage squatting on the flat deck of a dusty red four-wheel-drive.

'My God!' he breathed, his heart starting to race.

Warily, Hondelink moved closer to the back of the ute, making eye contact with one of the two black-and-white pigs. It glowered at him. These were not domestic pigs. Hondelink doubted very much if either the boar or the sow had seen a farmer's sty. They had too much hair, for one thing, and too much open belligerence.

Hondelink's eyes darted to the inside of the general store — no sign of the driver returning. With his mind in overdrive, mail and foodstuffs forgotten, he fished in a shirt pocket and found a ballpoint pen, then jotted down the vehicle's licence plate. Turning, he walked swiftly home.

One thing was certain: the red Toyota had to be the same vehicle that had been reported to him recently by Works roadmen on the road between

Makarora and Haast Pass as being used to transport pigs to the West Coast. Not once, either; on a number of occasions. He recalled helicopter pilot Alan Duncan's recent sighting of a pig in the Pleasant Flat area in the Landsborough River valley, as well as several nests in the tussock. Perhaps, Hondelink speculated, the driver of the red Toyota was involved with that liberation near Haast?

When the red ute pulled out of Hawea soon after and headed north along State Highway 6, it was trailed at a discreet distance by Paul Hondelink. He followed the vehicle to the start of the Haast Pass, where he pulled off the road, made a U-turn, and started back to Hawea. He was certain the driver hadn't stopped once. Just as well: in 1985 both he and John Fleming already had their hands full with liberated pigs.

Hondelink reported this incident to Forest Service personnel on the West Coast and checked out the number of the vehicle. The ute, he learned, belonged to a well-known North Otago runholder who had plenty of pigs on his land. Where was the sense to it?

Feral pigs have been established in several areas of the West Coast for many years. There have been many liberations, and the pigs are well settled in some sites around Karamea, Greymouth, Hokitika, Lake Paringa and Moeraki. DoC is working hard to wipe out some of the small, recently liberated mobs before they become established, particularly where they are a threat to wildlife such as giant land snails and penguins. The other concern to DoC is the fact that some of the pigs come from Otago, where bovine TB is endemic. Westland is TB-free south of Whataroa, and most of the farming in the area is cattle, highly vulnerable to TB.

Meantime there was plenty of government action on Mount Burke and Glen Dene stations. Paul Hondelink had supervised several hunting operations, to try and stop the build-up in numbers of pigs and prevent them moving north through The Neck into state forest, scenic reserve and Mount Aspiring National Park.

While there had been several reported sightings of wild pigs or pig sign on the western side of both Mount Burke and Glen Dene stations, the Lake Wanaka faces had yet to be inspected by the Forest Service. In March 1985, a five-man team from Queenstown was despatched to Mount Burke to work in close liaison with Hondelink and Fleming. The idea was that a larger group could give thorough coverage of the more difficult terrain; it would also enable the previously untouched lake faces to be surveyed. The team used a jet-boat, radios and a couple of pig-dogs. Twenty-seven pigs were taken in ten days, the bulk of them from the western Wanaka faces.

A total of 126 pigs had so far been taken in Forest Service operations. Cotty Burdon estimates station staff and private hunters accounted for between thirty and forty more. According to Paul Hondelink, until this time hunting pigs was not too difficult: they were generally quiet and in fine weather they liked nothing better than to lie in their nests in the sun-warmed fern. By following a leading ridge, it was often possible to observe them from a distance. In this situation, Hondelink found that the long-range capabilities of his .243 were of great benefit.

It couldn't last. The pigs became increasingly difficult to find, and more and more John Fleming came to rely on Mac's expertise in the art of locating and bailing pigs. Soon, Paul Hondelink acquired a pig-dog; there was no other way if they were going to come out on top. A hunter needs a dog or dogs to beat this most adaptable of adversaries.

In July 1987 pig control work continued on Glen Dene station and sixteen animals were destroyed, ten of which fell victim to helicopter pilot Doug Maxwell, who at the time was carrying out stock work. Meantime, pigs had turned up again on Cattle Flat station, where station staff observed six half-grown animals near the entrance to the Treble Cone ski field. They were last seen heading at a fast clip towards the station's boundary fence with Motatapu. Around this time, pig rooting was observed on Mount Albert station, on the western side of Lake Wanaka, near Makarora. The runholder, Jill Sarginson, contacted the Department of Conservation quickly and in due course John Fleming and Mac arrived on the scene.

As of 1 April 1987, the New Zealand Forest Service had ceased to exist; the Department of Conservation (DoC) now had the problem of wild animal control in this country. It made no difference to the feral pigs or, for that matter, to the Forest Service personnel. Only the name had changed — the work went on as before.

A Station Called Minaret

Minaret station, located rather neatly between West Wanaka and Mount Albert stations on the western shores of Lake Wanaka, covers 19,000 hectares. The station's mostly rugged terrain sweeps back from stock-dotted flatlands fronting the lake to a brutal mountain chain where several peaks exceed 2000 metres. With Cecil Peak and Halfway Bay stations — both situated on Lake Wakatipu — Minaret shares the distinction of being one of only three properties in the Southern Lakes district without road access.

The station receives on average 1500 millimetres of rain a year. This is far too damp for California quail but not for chuka, a hardy gamebird that is often observed at high altitudes. Chamois are comparatively common on the station and many a nice trophy has come from there. Like Mount Burke, the station was once alive with red deer, but today, again like the station across the lake, red deer are low in numbers and trophies are almost a thing of the past. There are no rabbits on Minaret; they were eliminated in 1955 following a concentrated effort by local runholders.

The Presland family have been on Minaret since 1950. Today Peter Presland, a tall, angular type with a sense of humour, and his wife Ann run the show with the assistance of a single shepherd. Without the benefit of road access, supplies and stock are brought in or taken out by a seven-metre barge built by Peter on the lines of World War II landing craft. As Ann says ruefully, it is a slow and often rough thirty-five kilometres from their jetty in Minaret Bay to Wanaka.

There is on Minaret station a wonderful sense of isolation, of being far removed from the rest of the world. This feeling is in no way undermined by the fact that they frequently use a helicopter to move stock and to gain access to, say, Dunedin, in double-quick time. Both Peter and Ann have long held helicopter pilot's licences; Ann won hers in 1973, the first woman in New Zealand to do so.

It was April 1989 and the blades of the Hughes 300 helicopter whipped through the air like a circular saw, whump-whump-whump! Like a gigantic dragonfly the machine banked sharply across the mountain-face; earth and sky merged and became one. The helicopter, the most versatile aircraft yet devised, levelled out and started its home run.

Peter Presland, a woollen-gloved hand relaxed on the cyclic control stick, was feeling well satisfied. He and his shepherd, Paul Corboy, had already put in a good day's work and it was barely past midday. They had gathered a mob of sheep up on the tops and worked them to lower ground. Another fall muster was going smoothly. A late lunch was in order; Peter would put a meal together quickly, something light. Normally Ann would have something warm ready, soup usually, but she was away on business.

They were descending quickly. Below, the lower slopes of the mountains, once covered with abundant beech forest, were dense with fern, bracken and manuka. They went down, low and fast, skimming a ridge, the powerful down-draught of the rotor making the carpet-like fern shake so violently it might have been lashed by a powerful storm.

Whump-whump-whump!

Suddenly, Peter looked surprised. Something strange back there — definitely not a chamois — was running through the fern. He half turned to Paul, a lean man in his late twenties.

'Good God!' Peter exclaimed. 'What the hell was that?'

Paul had also seen the puzzling movement. 'Dunno,' he muttered.

They went into a tight half-circle, the helicopter's Lycoming four-cylinder fuel-injected gasoline engine screaming as though in protest, the rotor blades chop-chopping through the air.

There! The high fern was moving, parting, ahead of them.

'Shit!' Paul cried. 'It's bloody pigs!'

Peter had a momentary but clear picture of two pigs running, one white, the other white with black spots. He was dumbfounded. Pigs? On Minaret? How on earth had they got here?

Grim faced, Peter headed for home. These intruders had to be dealt with today, while they knew where they were.

The helicopter touched down a short distance from the homestead. While Paul released the dogs from their cages on both skids and took them to their kennels, Peter, his mind in overdrive, raced to get his rifle. Pigs on Minaret? Quickly, they clambered into the helicopter. The engine was still running, the machine vibrating to its gutsy tune. They buckled their seatbelts and went aloft with Paul holding Peter's .308 rifle.

Nose down, they cut through a wide gap in a stand of exotic trees that had been there since Peter was a boy. The helicopter swung away from the lake, went past the homestead, and crossed a well-cropped paddock where red deer, contained by a high fence, gazed wistfully at the bush. Soon they touched down at a spot near to where they had observed the pigs. Peter killed the engine. The blades began to slow down, the machine ceased to vibrate; finally it squatted there like an ungainly winged toad.

With a light breeze blowing into their tense faces, they set off. There had been rain overnight and the fern was still damp. Peter moved quickly but with stealth. He had a gut feeling that the pigs would not have run too far before stopping and wondering what all the fuss was about.

The two men came across fresh rooting and a deeply concerned expression flooded Peter's face. Just how many pigs were there on the station? Well, he thought grimly, with luck there would shortly be two fewer. Fern brushed across his chest. To his surprise there was a lot of tension in him, seething, needing to escape. He felt angry too — these pigs were deliberately liberated on his land.

A pig grunted. The men stood stock still, hardly daring to breathe. Then Peter, half crouched, cut across to his right and suddenly saw them. They were the same pigs and they were rooting vigorously at the clump-like base of fern.

The racket of the .308 was awesome in its suddenness. A pig was down, lashing out frantically with its back legs; the other pig, stunned, pitched sideways to the ground as her mate kicked his last. A second shot rang out. The smell of sudden death hung in the air, warm and sweet. There were bright red patches of blood splashed on the white coats of the dead pigs; a few specks dabbed rather delicately on the fronds of emerald-green ferns.

The fallen animals were, Peter noted, a breeding pair. Anger came to the boil and he swore softly, potently. The pigs were in top condition; an autopsy would reveal they were free of TB. They would make fine eating.

When Ann heard about the pigs she was furious. How dare anyone do such a thing? Who did they think they were, these people? If they had to let pigs go, then why in God's name didn't they do it on their own land?

The next day, Peter and Paul worked back and forth — sometimes in the helicopter and sometimes on foot — over the area where they had killed the pigs. It was a broad area, perhaps as much as 1500 metres across, and they discovered extensive rooting. Could just two animals be responsible for this? Peter pondered. He decided it was possible.

Several weeks went by. The passenger's door of the helicopter was removed as though the Preslands had gone into the venison recovery business. When the machine was aloft, with either Peter or, mostly, Ann at the controls, it certainly looked as if they were deer shooting, with Paul sitting with Peter's .308 at the ready, peering out intently, praying to see an animal with bristle-like hair and a long snout perfectly designed for digging.

It was serious stuff on Minaret — top priority for the Preslands. The Hughes 300, having lost a door but gained a rifleman, became a familiar sight over sheltered, ferny hollows, ridges that caught the early morning sun and held it for many hours, and small clearings amidst the manuka scrub. But to the Preslands' profound relief they saw nothing to indicate the presence of more pigs on the station.

Meantime, they had had friends from North America stay. Ann served roast pork and vegetables for one evening meal, basic country fare dating back to the early settlers. The meal was a success, the meat tender and succulent, consistent with a young animal living mostly on the starch-rich roots of ferns. Perhaps they had had the last laugh, after all.

Two months later, Paul Hondelink received a telephone call of some significance. The caller told him that six, not two, pigs had been illegally liberated on Minaret station on 18 December 1988. The caller gave the liberation point, the person responsible and the makes of the vehicle and the boat used for transportation across the lake. He confirmed up to four illegal liberations by the same person within the last twelve months, within Minaret station, and on the Pisa Range and Mount Burke and Glen Dene stations.

Hondelink was concerned. Minaret had been pig-free country. If numbers were allowed to build up they could easily spread to Mount Aspiring National Park. He knew that pig liberations were still being made; in fact, it was quite an undercover industry. The accent was on improving the existing bloodlines and replacing stock taken from the wild. Pigs were being brought into the Central Otago region from around Te Anau and Catlins Forest Park, and, again, from a big, well-known station in Canterbury.

On a pleasant afternoon in late June, Ann was driving along the track near the lakefront at Snag Bay. She was close to the airstrip, just below a scrubby bench, when she saw something that caused her to brake violently. Fearing the worst, she sprang out of the four-wheel-drive.

At the homestead, Peter was making a pot of tea when he heard the Toyota pull up. Moments later, Ann stormed into the kitchen. She was flushed with anger as she explained that she had seen fresh pig rooting. Peter's shoulders slumped at the news. That was just what they needed!

That evening, armed with his .308, Peter went on foot to where Ann had told him the sign was. As he neared the area, he realised how much cover for a pig there was along the lakefront. Presently, he came to the rooting. He studied it, a rather perplexed expression on his craggy face. He had worked in the area for forty years. He recalled the plagues of rabbits, and the 100-strong herds of deer that ranged the run unchecked before the choppers moved in. He shook his head: the implications the rooting posed were enormous.

Peter went on, angling below the manuka bench. Suddenly he felt as though he were not alone. In mid stride he paused and, turning, peered into a wall of heavy, interlocked growth. His eyes narrowed. What was that? Gradually it took form, a dark, bulky shape, unmoving. His breath quickened. A boar!

Carefully, he raised his Parker Hale rifle, but the animal was too obscured, the chance that a bullet would be deflected too great. He held fire and breathed, 'Damn!' The boar was still, a statue. Warily, Peter took a few steps and then checked himself. The boar was aware of the man, had been for several minutes. Again Peter took aim, again it was too chancey.

Suddenly the boar spun about, fast, as if a dog was leaping at its throat. Unable to see it anymore, Peter darted after it. He heard a crash, the sounds of a heavy body breaking through the scrubby growth that plucked at his clothing and hindered his passage. The sounds faded to nothing and it was still. He knew he had blown it; a long, thin sigh escaped his lips.

Trudging home, Peter mulled over the incident. One thing was clear: this was not a semi-domesticated animal. This was the genuine article, a truly wild boar.

So the badly disgruntled Preslands took to the air again. Ann was quietly determined that she and a .308-toting Paul would be the combination to finally nail the boar. Day after day they scoured the low country. They used the same methods as the venison shooters: they hovered over likely cover, the landing skids almost touching the thick growth, the rotor blades beating the bushes and a siren going full blast.

Grimly, they searched for the boar from the air and on foot, but all to no avail. Indeed, they failed even to sight a single track or a clod of upturned earth. The boar seemed to have vanished, but they knew better than that: he was still there, somewhere.

So back and forth went the Hughes 300, thrashing the manuka, its siren screaming. Few, if any, deer are able to stand such pressure. Mostly they panic, and break wild-eyed into the open and a sudden burst of semi-automatic rifle fire. If death is not their lot, a net drops over them, bringing them crashing to the ground. But this was not a deer, this was a wild boar intelligent enough to hug the ground in deep cover when the ghastly creation was directly overhead. The trick was to wait it out, no matter how difficult that might be. Given time it always moved on.

In early June, Paul Corboy, wanting to buy a farm of his own, decided to leave Minaret and, much to the Preslands' regret, he handed in his notice. Two weeks later, Paul was in Wanaka, where he happened to meet up with an old mate, Kevin Henderson. Kevin, who came from North Canterbury, was a high-country musterer on the lookout for a job. Kevin had heard of Minaret and knew it was not linked to the outside world by road, something that appealed to the romantic side of his nature. Paul told him that Minaret was a great station and Peter Presland was a top bloke. In fact, Paul reckoned, Kevin couldn't do any better for himself than the station on the western side of Lake Wanaka.

That day, Kevin contacted Peter Presland, who interviewed him for the position of shepherd the following day. Peter warmed very quickly to the strongly built 24-year-old with the clean-cut looks, blue eyes and short-cropped blond hair. The job was Kevin's.

On the last day of July, Kevin started work on Minaret. In the afternoon Peter decided to see if they could locate the boar. Kevin, of course, had heard about the pigs, first from Paul and then from Peter. The mere thought of hunting from the air was more than enough to set Kevin's heart racing. Peter well understood that sort of passion; he had, in fact, been under its influence most of his life.

When Kevin swung his compact body into the cockpit of the Hughes 300 he was carrying a brand-new .243 Browning rifle, fitted with a 4x Tasco scope. He would have much preferred to have been using his old .444 Marlin — the lever-action piece with its much heavier cartridge was more suitable for close-range stuff in thick growth — but the rear sight had been broken in transit a few days ago. No matter. A 100-grain slug would not prove lacking.

The Hughes 300 clattered into the air; Kevin clutched his rifle. Presently, Peter pointed below.

'Snag Bay — that's where the liberations took place, I believe.'

Kevin bobbed his head.

They remained aloft for around half an hour. The sleek Browning had yet to claim its first victim. Later, in his quarters, Kevin mulled over Peter's parting words: sooner or later someone would see the boar and they should carry their rifles at all times. Kevin had no objections; life on Minaret, he thought, was off to a fine start.

A week or so after he had arrived on Minaret, Kevin stumbled across concrete evidence that the boar was not a figment of the Preslands' imagination. The clear-cut tracks on the pebbly beach to the south of Snag Bay were those of a mature pig all right. Kevin was galvanised into action and he spent several icy-cold evenings looking for the boar in the vicinity. Again the boar proved elusive.

It was late August when a sickly ewe gave up the ghost and died on the flats below the airstrip. No one took much notice — death in winter was part and parcel of station life. It was Mother Nature's brutal but essential culling programme. Perhaps a week later Peter, flying over these same flats, noticed that the obviously rotting carcass had been disturbed. He caught his breath as he went in for a closer look. Wool was scattered about the carcass . . . something had been feeding on it.

On 30 August, at the end of a lovely winter's day, Kevin stood hands on hips, looking over his handiwork. Tendril-like columns of smoke drifted from the smouldering hillside after a burnoff to check the rampant fern. Time to call it a day, he realised with satisfaction. His two sheepdogs — Joe, a black-and-tan huntaway and Flea, a collie bitch — were sitting nearby. Whenever he could, Kevin gave his dogs a run.

Thinking about the boar, he reached the Toyota and drove the short distance to the end of the airstrip. From this point there was a good view of the flats. Using a miniature pair of 7 x 21 field-glasses, he examined the lakefront. Nothing that even remotely resembled a pig. Hmm . . . the boar wouldn't be too far away; he was probably camped near what remained of the ewe's carcass. He heard a distant helicopter. That would be Ann; she had gone to Wanaka for the day. The sound grew louder.

Shrugging, Kevin pocketed his field-glasses. He was just about to drive off when at the extreme edge of his field of vision he spotted a movement. It was at the far end of the flats, at least a mile away. Shading his eyes, the better to see against the lowering sun, he still couldn't see exactly what was running towards cover. Nevertheless, he had a pretty good idea even before he snapped the glasses to his eyes. He sucked in his breath sharply.

A boar was running pell-mell; the tempo of the Hughes 300, increasing by the second, seemed to spur the boar on even faster. The black-and-white animal was fairly flying over the ground.

Grabbing his rifle, Kevin set off at a hard run, his dogs beside him. A fence loomed up. Rifle slung, Kevin hardly broke stride as he grabbed the top of a wooden post and vaulted it like a gymnast. Flea, a slip of a dog, sailed cleanly between the wide-spaced wires but Joe, considerably bigger and much less agile, was momentarily caught up in the wires before breaking free. One of the wires carried an electric current and, to judge by Joe's sudden agonised yelp, the power was on. Kevin looked apprehensively over his shoulder but Joe was still mobile, determined to keep up like all good huntaways.

By this time, of course, the boar had vanished. Kevin could only hope it didn't go too far. It seemed hopeless — still, he had to try. At last he came to a stop where he had seen the boar dash into the manuka. To his amazement, he saw that the boar hadn't gone at all. It was there, just inside the barrier of scrub, staring at him.

Shakily, Kevin raised his rifle. The barrel wobbled as he tried to get his ragged breathing under control. Willing the round home, he pressed rather than touched the trigger. The .243 cracked viciously. The boar grunted as it spun about. The dogs, gun shy, rushed trembling to their master's feet. A spent cartridge blurred as it flashed over Kevin's shoulder and, as he thrust a replacement into the breach, it didn't seem possible that he had missed from no more than thirty metres.

Quickly now, trying to regain his shattered composure, he dashed after the boar and for a second time he was amazed. It was there, dead. Grinning broadly, he looked at the .243's first kill. The boar's tusks were of reasonable, but not trophy, length; it weighed around 198 pounds on the hoof. One thing was absolutely certain. The Preslands were going to be delighted when they heard the news.

The TB Dilemma

It was in the winter of 1989 that runholders and farmers in the Upper Clutha, especially those on the Pisa and Criffel Ranges, first discovered that the rumour of bovine tuberculosis in pigs in the Central Otago district was not idle speculation but harsh reality. The ramifications were of concern to anyone in the area who ran cattle or deer.

John Aspinall was secretary of the local branch of Federated Farmers at the time. 'Until that particular winter we hadn't realised that pigs carried TB. It was only when Richard Snow of Morven Hills shot thirty-odd pigs on his place and sent them to Mossburn Game Packing House that the trouble really started — about one-third of them were confirmed carriers of TB.'

In August Aspinall convened a meeting of the Upper Clutha branch of Federated Farmers to discuss the TB problem. As a result of the meeting he wrote to the Ministry of Agriculture and Fisheries to find out what they planned to do. MAF was able to confirm that it had been known for some time that feral pigs in the Lindis area were infected with bovine TB, but that no work had been done to determine the rate of infection or even whether or not pigs could transmit the disease to stock. The only action MAF was prepared to take was to release some money to help pay for the eradication of feral pigs, and to research the role of pigs in the transfer of infection.

In a four-page colour brochure sent to the committee, MAF does recommend hunters check for TB by looking for swollen glands under the jaw, which may have a whitish fluid seeping from them. These lesions often feel gritty when cutting through them. MAF asks that if you find a suspected TB pig, you place the 'suspicious' pieces in a plastic bag and store them in a cool place without freezing, then contact MAF. The leaflet warns that humans can become infected from handling an infected pig, so care should be taken to disinfect or sterilise all knives and instruments used, wash hands thoroughly and disinfect clothing and footwear.

In September 1989 MAF and DoC combined forces in a helicopter and ground shoot in the Pisa, Cardrona and Criffel areas. In December of the same year the local 'Pig Committee' met to discuss progress so far. It was reported that 137 pigs had been shot of which 95 were post-mortemed; 31 were found to have bovine TB. All the TB pigs had come from one of three mobs: it was clear to the committee that there was some transfer of the disease within the pig population, and possibly to other species. However, of the 160 goats, 184 possums, 283 rabbits, a couple of ferrets and a cat shot on the same campaign, not one was found to have TB.

The committee resolved to keep pig disturbance to a minimum during autumn, so that the pigs would regroup and settle. Then, following a good snowfall, the remaining pigs would be surveyed from a helicopter and then shot or poisoned. Funding was arranged through MAF, and two local vets, Richard Bishop and Gary Walker, offered to check pig carcasses for TB free of charge. The committee noted that there was some incidence of TB in cattle herds in areas where there was a high rate of infection among pigs, and believed that it would be possible to eradicate the disease in the area by eliminating the feral pig population.

Not surprisingly, this sort of approach is not popular with pig-hunters. They claim that to kill the entire pig population is an over-reaction; most pigs don't carry TB, and anyway there is little to suggest that deer and cattle can catch TB from feral pigs. Gary Knowles of MAF is difficult to pin down on the subject. When I visited him in his office in 1990 I asked him a pertinent question.

'Where do wild pigs get TB from?'

Gary smiled disarmingly. 'We simply don't know.'

I nodded. 'Can it be stated conclusively that feral pigs transmit TB to farm animals?'

Gary's smile was working overtime. 'At this stage we don't know the answer to that one, either.'

'So how come the pig is being made the villain?'

'Is it?' replied Gary in his best public servant voice. If you don't want to make waves, you go with the flow.

Gary paused thoughtfully, then went on. 'Overseas research — mainly from Australia, I think — suggests that feral pigs are simply hosts of TB, and once they contract it, the disease goes no further.'

'So the research goes on?'

'Absolutely!'

Is Anywhere Safe?

The undulating Kaitake Range lies north-west of the distinctive 2518-metre cone of Mount Egmont, better known these days as Taranaki. Part of Egmont National Park, the Kaitake Range, rising to 683 metres, is all that remains of the Kaitake volcano, which during its active period about 500,000 years ago may have been as high as Taranaki is now. The Kaitake Range covers 1600 hectares. The steep upper slopes and almost all of the peaks are covered with kamahi, while the lower forest is mostly tawa.

Red deer have never found their way into Egmont National Park, but wild goats have been there a very long time. They have been hunted extensively by Forest Service and, later, DoC hunters; they pose a far greater threat to the environment than any species of deer.

Until 1988 wild pigs had never been a problem in Egmont National Park. Surprising, bearing in mind that Taranaki is a major hunting province. The Park Board and DoC wanted very much for that situation to remain unchanged, but with so many liberations taking place around the country, they harboured fears for their particular patch.

Major problems would arise if pigs were liberated in the park. Conservation Officer Kerry Matthews highlights some of them:

> Pigs, if they became established, would threaten the survival of the park's endemic snail; they would disturb the ground cover and thus provide suitable sites for weed invasion. Native birds and insects would have competition for food, particularly fallen fruit from species such as kohekohe and tawa. The areas favoured by kiwi would also provide choice sites for pigs.
>
> By continually providing disturbed ground, pigs have the potential to alter the successional sequences that have had such a major influence on the pattern of vegetation present in the park. In the extensive subalpine shrublands, grasslands and the Ahukawakawa

swamp, pigs have the potential to have a serious impact on many of the herbaceous species that exist under the woody vegetation or in association with tussocks.

Pigs are also cited as a major threat to farm animals in and around the park. Pigs are very susceptible to bovine TB and any animal liberated in the park could easily be carrying this disease, especially if it had been caught in the wild. Bovine TB is not known from any wild animals on the Taranaki ring plain, but it is common in possums and pigs further east towards Taumarunui. If TB was spread via pigs to the possum population of Egmont National Park, eradication of the disease would be a costly and perhaps impossible exercise. The TB-free status of Taranaki could in the future be a major asset to the region if major markets around the world insist that dairy products they import come from TB-free areas.

As well as the ecological and stock health reasons against liberation of pigs on Egmont anybody considering such an act should bear in mind the provisions of the law. Under the Wild Animal Control Act and the National Parks Act it is an offence to liberate animals. The penalties can be severe, for example, the National Parks Act provides for imprisonment for up to three months or a fine up to $2500. If the offence is committed by a corporation the fine can be up to $25,000. The offender is liable for all the costs associated with removing the animals and repairing the damage done. On land managed under the Conservation Act the fines can be even more severe, up to $10,000 for an individual and $80,000 for a corporation.

In July 1988, while on wild goat control operations, DoC hunter Heath Priest came across an unexpected sight — the random, fresh rootings of what he presumed was a young boar of about 60–70 pounds. Priest wasted little time in relaying this information to his boss, Kerry Matthews, pinpointing the exact spot on a map. The deeply worried Matthews nodded thoughtfully as he studied it: East Ridge, above Whenuariki Stream, directly behind the property of Matt Redshaw.

Kerry Matthews acted quickly, visiting the area on a number of occasions to discover where and how many they were, and how much damage had been done. He was able to estimate that there were around fifteen feral pigs; it was evident that these animals were breeding.

The area in which the pigs were living, on the north-western and western slopes of the Kaitake Range, is classified as semi-coastal forest — generally low-lying, warm, sheltered and abundantly watered. Apart from the dominant tawa, sub-canopy species such as pigeonwood, pukatea, mahoe and silver fern flourish in this environment. Gully bottoms are thick with supplejack and kiekie; the soil is rich in insect life and juvenile root systems. This was ideal habitat for feral pigs.

It was obvious that instant eradication of the feral pigs was necessary.

However, the local Department hunters did not have trained pig-dogs, and Matthews feared that their efforts might not be fully effective and could educate the animals to hunting pressure and encourage them to spread over a much wider area. Instead Matthews engaged the assistance of two particularly experienced pig-hunters with fully trained and regularly worked dogs.

The hunters quickly accounted for six young sows, an older sow thought to be their mother, a young boar and three piglets. All were in excellent condition. It was good to know that so many had been shot, but Kerry Matthews was still worried about ranging animals establishing new populations elsewhere in the park. The more mobs there were, and the wider they were scattered, the harder they would be to control. Meantime the hunters continued their work; by the end of April 1990 they had shot thirty-two more pigs, including five pregnant sows.

For ten weeks in the autumn and winter of 1990 a DoC hunter also battled the elements and the dense undergrowth, but his return was meagre: only four pigs. Obviously ten weeks in the Kaitake Range chasing elusive pigs was more than enough for him: shortly afterwards he handed in his notice.

Determined not to allow the pressure to ease, Kerry Matthews sought the services of a very experienced pig-hunter, Peter Miscall. He would be employed initially on a two-month contract. Miscall had gained his hard-won knowledge of pigs in North Taranaki, especially the Whangamomona district, where wild pigs were an accepted part of the community. Generally speaking, the forests that Miscall had hunted were much more open than that which clothed the Kaitake Range and at first his dogs had problems adapting. Nevertheless they and Miscall persisted.

Peter Miscall kept a hunting diary while he was in the Kaitake Range. These extracts give an idea of his successes and frustrations:

> **11 June** Lost a good pig in the head of the Wairau Stream gully.
> **13 June** Got onto mob of pigs high in the Wairau Stream gully, left fork. Due to rough country dogs beaten again — missing for three hours.
> **18 June** Caught 60-pound sow carrying 5 piglets, age approximately 12 months old, not bad condition.
> **20 June** Lost dog on pigs above Hewer's property — picked them up next day.
> **29 June** Caught 80-pound sow carrying 7 piglets, aged 2–3 years in average condition. Bloody wet all day!
> **3 July** 70-pound sow, 6 piglets inside, in good condition, age approximately 3 years old.
> **6 July** 100-pound boar, razorback. Bloody toey — fought dogs for $^{3}/_{4}$ hour, finally stopped him halfway down from ridge tops between Davis Track and the Pikiwati Stream.

10 July Caught 80-pound sow carrying 6 piglets; also 60-pound boar; dogs had another one but killed it before I arrived. Pigs were rooting on Telford's farm during the night.
18 July 70-pound Tammy [Tamworth] boar 12–18 months old, average condition; also 70-pound sow carrying 6 piglets, in poor condition. Animals caught end of Wairau Road above farmland behind gum trees.
25 July 70-pound sow carrying 6 piglets, sow in fat condition. Lost dogs heading in Wairau Gully direction. I'd say they killed another pig as I picked them up on dark at the top of Wairau Road.
31 July 100-pound sow carrying 5 piglets; sow in good condition. Dogs bailed her way up Nursery Gully. Broke from dogs, ran out into farmland. Shot in farm gully.
3 August Two 70-pound boars, average condition, 18 months old. One in the head of the Wairau Stream and the other on Kerry's hunting track.

Meantime, Kerry Matthews was checking out the damage, and found some areas where the pig rooting 'resembled a random ploughing operation'. This was particularly a problem in the bush terraces between 180 metres and 330 metres where nikau palm was predominant: feral pigs love the roots of the nikau. Otherwise, the damage was scattered.

Matthews was astounded at the rate the pigs were breeding and wondered if they were trying to quickly establish in new territory following release, as has happened with many feral animal populations, most notably red deer. But there wasn't time for theorising. Total eradication was the aim and, although it was proving very difficult to achieve, Miscall was learning fast. He found that the pigs not destroyed were regrouping and often relocating to a familiar area, usually a gully or bush face. The hunter only had to return to these areas to get results. If Peter Miscall was unsure where the pigs had moved to he simply walked through the area without dogs to find them.

By 17 December 1990, Peter Miscall and his dogs had eliminated a further twenty-two pigs, among them a 120-pound boar, another boar of 100 pounds, and a pregnant sow carrying eight piglets. This brought the grand total of pigs destroyed since DoC operations had started to seventy-nine animals, with a further forty-five young being found in pregnant sows. It seemed the pigs were almost done for. Kerry Matthews reported that all that remained was a boar and perhaps six juveniles. These pigs were proving harder to track down, perhaps because of what they had learned from the past hunting pressure. Peter Miscall was spending a great deal of time tracking the remaining pigs without success, and after Christmas he transferred to feral goat control.

When Peter Miscall's stint as a seasonal hunter in the Kaitake Range came to an end in April 1991, there was still an unknown number of wild pigs in the area. It was a bitter pill for Conservation Officer Kerry Matthews to swallow; his thoughts will strike a chord with anyone who cares about Egmont National Park.

> What have we got to lose if pigs are successfully established in Egmont National Park?
>
> To guess at what there is to lose you need an appreciation of what is special about this part of New Zealand. Mount Taranaki and its associated peaks of the Pouakai and Kaitake Ranges are clothed in a complex pattern of vegetation that has its like nowhere else in the world. Each of the peaks is the centre of its own botanical district whose plant make-up is strongly influenced by the length of time since the last eruption of the mountain. The Kaitake Range is the oldest of the three and Taranaki itself the youngest. Within each of these major time periods there have been other eruption sequences of a lesser nature and these have contributed to the complex pattern of successional vegetation types that are visible today.
>
> The park contains the only substantial stands of lowland and semi-coastal forest remaining on the Taranaki volcanic ring plain. The rest has been cleared for farming. As well as its unique patterns of vegetation the park contains several rare species of plant including one in the mahoe family that is found nowhere else. The Ahukawakawa swamp, between Mount Taranaki and the Pouakai Range is the only known site for six species in the North Island.
>
> The park has its own species of large land snail, *Powelliphanta* 'Egmont' and a rare giant amphipod (hopper), *Tara taranaki*. The park is also rich in Maori archaeological sites. Pa, food pits, midden and urupa are among the known sites.

During the latter part of 1991, Kerry Matthews visited the areas where pigs had been previously observed in the Kaitake Range and reached the conclusion that only two pigs were still there, two sows of around 80–90 pounds. At the time I contacted Kerry Matthews, it was DoC's intention to call in the services of Peter Miscall in early 1992 to eliminate the remaining animals. By then, however, if the sows were pregnant, he may be dealing with more than two pigs.

The question, of course, remains as to who liberated pigs here in the first instance. While Kerry Matthews might never know the answer to that, he is quite certain of one thing: he does not want a repeat performance.

Wild Pork!

In February 1989, Graham Nugent, a scientist with the Forest Animal Ecology group (Forest Research Institute, Christchurch), produced a four-page questionnaire on hunting in New Zealand, which was posted to 9940 people chosen at random from the 324,075 firearms licensees at the time; around 88 percent of the big-game hunters and 78 percent of the gamebird hunters sent in detailed replies. Separate postal surveys were also made of commercial big-game hunters, including helicopter operators involved in wild-animal recovery.

The survey concluded that there were about 20,500 ground-based pig-hunters in the country, that they hunted on average fifteen times a year, and for their troubles took five pigs apiece. All up they accounted for about 100,000 pigs. Most hunters then retained their kills; some would have no doubt given the odd carcass to a mate, others would have sold them in hotels. However, at least 14,000 wild pig carcasses were sold to firms such as Game Recovery of Renwick.

In 1988 Game Recovery, part of Dunedin-based Tanimax Trading and Main Astley Ltd, had twenty-eight chiller depots in the country, most in the top half of the South Island. In fact, the company handled most of the wild pigs offered for sale in Marlborough. Game Recovery in 1988 paid hunters $1.50 per kilogram for head-shot animals and $1.00 per kilogram for those shot elsewhere. Because of strict health regulations, Game Recovery only purchased animals shot over the weekend. They had to weigh in excess of 56 pounds, be accompanied by their vital organs and offal, chilled within ten hours of death, and taken early in the week by refrigerated truck to Westland Frozen Products' factory at Hokitika. There, within seventy-two hours of being chilled, they had to be inspected by a qualified meat inspector. Needless to say, the pigs were processed under strict hygiene regulations.

Wakefield-based Cyril Heywood had been an ardent pig-hunter for thirty-eight years and in his teens hunted pigs for a bounty. Hunters in the 1950s were paid one shilling for the snout and tail of any wild pig and were also rewarded with three rounds of .303 ammunition. There were, of course, ways to improve one's bounty and, according to an interview Heywood gave to the *Weekend Star* (Christchurch), he and his roguish companions once opened up the gut of a pregnant sow and took the tails and snouts of the unborn pigs, too. A case of Kiwi ingenuity, right?

The biggest boar Cyril Heywood can recall seeing was ranging a station in the upper Wairoa Valley, Nelson. Hunters Snow Hebberd of Raglan and Blue Hebberd of Picton combined forces to take out the animal after dark. It weighed 275 pounds. Cyril Heywood's brother, Ian, was a notable pig-hunter too. Over a two-month period at Port Gore, Marlborough, he once took four tonnes of wild pork.

So, in the early part of 1988 things were going smoothly for Tanimax Trading's diversification into the exportation of wild pork. They were processing about eighty carcasses a week and were hoping that hunters would sell them about 2000 carcasses over the year. Of this projected figure, 1500 would be sent to Europe, mainly West Germany and France. Once it reaches Europe, all New Zealand wild pork is sold as wild boar meat. It has long been a traditional dish in that part of the world, dating from a time when hardy men used nets and spears and half-wild dogs the size of wolves to bring down the fearsome wild boar. The majority of wild pork exported to Europe, where it is much more expensive than domestic pig meat, is sold in work-place cafeterias.

Then, suddenly, sales of wild New Zealand pork to Europe slumped. Why? In a word, Chernobyl. The biggest nuclear power disaster of all time had far-reaching tentacles. The problem was that the local consumer could not tell the difference between local wild boar meat, believed contaminated by what had happened at Chernobyl, and meat imported from New Zealand.

In 1987 the following article appeared in the *Christchurch Star* under the headline 'Wild pigs top mercury levels':

> Unsafe mercury levels have been unexpectedly found in wild pigs and the Health Department has warned consumers not to eat wild pork more than once a week.
>
> The surprise results followed what experts thought would be a routine follow-up to testing of domestic pigmeat.
>
> The acting director general of the Ministry of Agriculture and Fisheries, Mr Royce Elliot, said the ministry was still assessing what action it should take to make sure domestic sales and exports of the pork complied with Health Department safety levels.
>
> Levels in the pigs' offal, which includes liver, kidney and heart, were 0.27 parts a million — nine times over the Health Department's food tolerance level of 0.03 parts a million.

The manager of health protection for the Health Department, Mr John Stephenson, said wild pork consumption patterns in New Zealand were not known.

About $500,000 worth of wild pork is exported each year and Dr Stephenson said there was concern overseas buyers might link the problem with wild pork to other game meat produced in New Zealand.

High results were found following checks on pigs from west coast of South Island, Rotorua and Taupo.

During his extensive research into wild pigs in the northern half of the South Island in 1987 and 1988, Colin Clarke of the Forest Research Institute in Christchurch gathered material that proved wild pigs are now found over half of this huge region. He found that the heaviest concentrations of pigs were in Marlborough, around Murchison, and on D'Urville Island. The most common colour of pigs was black, with other animals grey-blue, white, brown-tan, or ginger-red.

Clarke found by questioning experienced pig-hunters that recreational hunters were having an increasingly important part to play in the control of feral animals in New Zealand. Experienced pig-hunters were defined as owning or having access to a pack of pig-dogs; approximately 40 percent of the pig-hunters involved belonged to pig-hunting clubs. They tended to be employed in seasonal occupations such as shearing, freezing work, farming and forestry, or other forms of employment such as driving trucks or working as linesmen. Clearly the sport attracted a certain outdoor type rather than a cross-section of society. Most pig-hunters contacted were aged between twenty and forty. More than half had more than ten years' experience, with an overall average of eighteen years afield. Impressive.

Clarke was able to conclude from the survey that pig-hunting, unlike other forms of hunting, was experiencing an upswing in popularity. Hunters were prepared to travel to hunt; Canterbury hunters travelled the furthest, many making the rough-trip to Nelson or Marlborough (at the time of the survey dogs were banned from most DoC land in Canterbury). These experienced pig-hunters hunted on average fifty days a year; each hunter killed on average fifty-seven pigs. The most successful hunter took a staggering 364. Most hunters agreed that to make it worthwhile maintaining a pig-dog pack they needed to take, say, twenty pigs a year.

An estimated 40,000–50,000 pigs were taken during the year in question from the top half of the South Island, most from privately owned farmland. While DoC land was estimated to carry 37 percent of the overall pig population, it received only 26 percent of hunter effort and yielded a mere 14 percent of the annual harvest. Even a fairly dozy pig would realise the advantages of residing on DoC land. Of the experienced pig-hunters who had been on DoC land, 86 percent considered they had been badly hampered by restrictions being placed on the numbers of dogs used.

PART TWO

Mostly Boars and Pig-dogs

The wild bunch, Turangi, October 1984: Keri Duff, Moss Albert, Manu Edwards, Darkie Duff, Colin 'Bing' Albert, Pat Tahi and Manu Jensen.

Turangi Interlude

On a fine spring afternoon in the October of 1984, I drove into Taupo, en route to Turangi, where I intended to spend a couple of days simply relaxing. Soon I drew level with the turn-off to Napier — State Highway 5, a 90-minute run to Hawke's Bay.

Memories, huh? Some were lovely, some plain lousy, but they are all a part of life, right? Now, as I put the turn-off behind me, I could see in my mind's eye two young, super-fit government shooters waiting for a lift on the side of the road. Angus Thompson and I had had a weekend in town and were heading back to a small hut on the eastern fringes of Kaingaroa Forest. That was early 1962, as I recall. Eighteen quid a week to nail deer and pigs.

Twenty-three years later, I made camp at a motel in Turangi. Located at the southern end of the largest lake in the country, Turangi has always seemed to me to be in Taupo's shadow. Yet for an outdoor holiday it possibly surpasses Taupo: deer and pigs within easy reach, rivers and, of course, the lake to fish in, rapids to rampage down in overgrown rubber dinghies, tracks to tramp, horses to ride.

On the western edge of town, on the road to Tokaanu, I had noticed a likely looking place that hired out horses. A quick check of the telephone directory and I had the number. A deep voice on the other end of the line belonged to one Darkie Duff. Yeah, they had good horses and saddles. Why didn't I come out and see for myself right now?

Gunning along State Highway 1, I looked south to a distinct 1325-metre peak named Pihanga, bathing in the evening sun. The mountain is towards the eastern end of a long stretch of forested country bisected by State Highway 47 — Turangi to National Park — and pigs range all through it. The locals have taken some top boars in that particular country, some within sight of Turangi.

I reached my destination, a large, railed yard, within a few minutes. It contained several good-looking nags, with nosebags in place. A small dark mare was being groomed by a tall man wearing jeans and rubber boots. Darkie Duff? As I slipped through the wooden rails a couple of horses gave me an unconcerned once-over; a big dog, stretched out on a dirty saddle blanket, stood up, shook himself with vigour, and shot me a penetrating look. It growled deep in its ample chest; it sounded like thunder breaking ominously over Pihanga. I decided I wasn't too keen on the dog.

'Boofy!' the man snapped.

Dog shut up.

Boofy? I wondered. I mean, this was one battle-scarred, ugly-as-sin, powerful-looking brute; the kind of canine that could shit bricks and flash you a toothy grin while doing it.

The man said with a reassuring smile, 'Don't worry yourself — he won't hurt ya.'

'But he could if he wanted to,' I pointed out.

'Shit, yeah!'

This tall, bearded character was indeed Darkie Duff. He was a lean, muscular type in his mid-thirties, with long dark hair shot with streaks of grey, and the kind of hard, wary face you might associate with one of Te Kooti's band.

We talked about trivial matters for a couple of minutes and then he said, 'You ride OK?'

'Good enough not to need supervision.'

Darkie nodded at a chestnut mare of maybe fifteen hands.

'Lady'll do ya.' He added that she was eight years old and had, like a lot of horses in the area, originated from wild stock once common in the local national park.

Lady, I thought, looked very special and it was obvious that there was something apart from brumby blood in her lineage. Darkie confirmed that she had been crossed with a quarter horse along the way, hence her chunky build, and that there was a bit of Arab blood mixed in there, too.

'So ten o'clock's OK?' I said, ready to leave him to his grooming.

'Yeah.' Again he gave me a thoughtful look; he'd been doing that off and on ever since I had introduced myself. 'Hey!' He snapped a thumb and forefinger together. 'You the fella wrote that book on pigs?'

I confirmed it with a nod. Darkie digested the information with the sort of expression that could turn into a warm smile or, just as likely, a ferocious scowl. Suddenly, he smiled with genuine warmth; it transformed his face completely.

'Bloody good book, that one.'

'Thanks,' I said, meaning it.

'Most of the fellas around here've got it.'

I left Darkie Duff grooming his neat little mare, Millie Small.

The next day provided a wonderful spring morning of perhaps twenty humidity-free degrees. There was a strong aroma of wild broom in the air and as I arrived at my destination at 9.45 I had a lovely feeling that spring would turn to summer and that all the horrible cold and wet stuff was many months away.

There was activity at the horse yard: five men and a young woman were rubbing down and saddling horses. Dogs were lolling about, Boof-head included. No prizes for guessing what Boofy's mates were — pig-dogs through and through. Darkie Duff was sorting gear at the tack shed.

'Handle a western saddle OK?'

'Sure thing.' I used a Mexican or roping saddle a great deal when I lived in Australia.

Laughter rang out from the horse yard.

'Who's the wild bunch?' I jerked a thumb.

Darkie grinned. 'That's the welcoming committee.'

'Eh?' I said blankly.

Darkie again bared his teeth. 'Hope you don't mind, Phil, but I spread the word that you were in town and they all wanna go riding with you.' With me? 'C'mon,' Darkie added, and strode towards the horse yard.

In turn I was introduced to them all. Keri Duff, Darkie's sister, gave me a shy smile and then went on grooming her horse. Manu Edwards was a slim guy in a hooped rugby shirt and a rolled-up balaclava. Colin 'Bing' Albert was heavy-set, attired in a thick woollen shirt and wearing a peaked cap. Solidly built Pat Tahi was in a good old bushman's Swanndri and shaded his eyes with a peaked cap. Moss Albert wore a football jersey with the insignia of a springbok on it; his woollen hat had a piece missing off the front. Manu Jensen was sensibly attired in an army-type jungle-green shirt. Later I learned that they were all more or less related to each other.

Presently, we mounted up. They were all fine-looking horses and, as we started out at a jog, it was obvious the wild bunch could all ride well, too. I was delighted with Lady, and the top-notch locally made saddle was comfort itself. Old times, I reckon. Now, stirrup to stirrup with Darkie as we followed a slushy track through tall stands of broom, I was told that all except Keri had just returned from a two-week trip that had taken them into wild country in the headwaters of the Wanganui River. They had taken fifteen horses, some as spare mounts or for carrying supplies. They had taken a few basics — bread, butter, salt and tea — and the rest of their food came from the land in the form of venison, pork and eels.

'We get away pretty often,' Darkie said, adjusting the brim of his floppy straw hat. 'Does you good, eh?'

I glanced down at Boofy trotting alongside; Boofy looked happy. I noticed the scars criss-crossing his coat.

'Been in the wars, eh?'

Darkie bobbed his head and laughed with gallows humour. 'Hell, yeah! Some mean pigs around here and he's met most of 'em head on!'

'Patch him up yourself?'

'Sometimes, if he's not too badly hurt. Been to the local vet a few times, though. They're real good mates by now.'

It was, I mused, difficult to pinpoint Boofy's lineage, which is nothing unusual where pig-dogs are concerned. Certainly his solid build and menacing looks stamped him as some sort of a guard dog.

Darkie explained. 'He's a Rottweiler/bull-terrier/Labrador cross.'

'Some combination!'

'Right! Bugger doesn't know when to back off, y'know. Might get him killed one day.'

'Take a good boar to do that.'

'Sure, but like I've said, they're around.'

There were two more dogs out for a run and, like Boofy, they were revelling in it. Tupe was a young Dobermann/Labrador cross and Brownie was a Rhodesian ridgeback/Labrador cross. Both were good-looking animals.

Darkie suddenly changed the subject. 'Married?'

'Separated.' I paused, my mood reflective. 'You?'

Darkie shook his head with vigour. 'Naw — but I sure put in a helluva lot of practice!'

Later, I linked up with Colin, a nice, easy-going type in his thirties. He had a top roping saddle and his mare, Kate, was a splendid animal. I said as much and he smiled with pleasure and said she came from the national park high country, apparently known for top animals. Curious, I asked Colin what they all did for a living; it was, after all, a week day. Colin said they took what work they could find, which, since unemployment was a real problem in Turangi, wasn't much. Darkie, for instance, a bushman from way back, broke horses, did some stock work on local stations or trapped possums.

'We get away hunting a lot,' Colin said. He gestured broadly, taking in Pihanga and a sweep of wild country. 'Good life, eh?' He smiled and looked relaxed, the way few city folk are.

It was, I mused, not a bad life for Darkie and Colin and their mates. The longer I remained in their company that day, the more I enjoyed it.

Finally, I said to Colin, 'It was real nice of you guys to come out with me. Appreciate it.'

Colin nodded thoughtfully and indicated the others as they bunched together. 'They respect you. That book you wrote gave you mana.'

In my forty-sixth year I was more than willing to settle for that.

That afternoon the sweat-darkened animals, saddles removed, were again brushed and generally pampered. A mixture of corn, maize and barley was tipped into feed bins. Tupe, inclined to wander, was secured by a length of rope to one of the horses' tails, Brownie was sunbathing, and big, scowling Boofy had ambled off to lie in the shade of the tack shed.

Three pig-dogs, then, which were a pretty successful blending of five different breeds: Rottweiler, Dobermann, bull-terrier, Rhodesian ridgeback and Labrador. The Rottweiler and Dobermann fell into the

On the eastern side of the Pisa Range, on Mount Pisa station.

Lochaburn station homestead.

John Fleming and Meg on Glen Dene station.

Cotty Burdon, Mount Burke.

Jerry Burdon, Glen Dene.

Willie 'Wong' Cowie glassing for pigs on Bendigo station.

Paul Hondelink, DoC.

John Aspinall, Mount Aspiring.

Looking across Lake Wanaka to Minaret station (directly behind Peter Presland's helicopter). The station has no road access, which did not stop an illegal release of pigs.

Kevin Henderson, shepherd on Minaret station.

working dog group although they were not, as such, working dogs; the bull-terrier, a member of the twenty-four strong terrier group, was a sporting breed; the Rhodesian ridgeback belonged to the hound group and, again, was a sporting breed; the Labrador was, specifically, a gundog.

Most pig-hunters have their favourite breed of dog. Boofy, for instance, in temperament and appearance, was predominantly Rottweiler. Basically, pig-dogs are classified into three specific groups: finders, bailers and holders. There are, of course, dogs that find and hold; money couldn't buy them. Long-term finders would, I suspect, never mix it with an irate boar, for that is the role of the straight-out holder, a dog with more than a generous measure of guts, tenacity and the ability to soak up heaps of punishment. It goes without saying that a lightly built border collie is not strong or gutsy enough to act as a holder.

The most likely ancestor of the dog is the wolf — not just the European wolf but several types of wolves, among them the Chinese wolf, the North American wolf and the Indian plains wolf. Around 10,000 to 12,000 years ago, in a period of immense change, some races of people adopted a more stable and sedentary way of life, allowing them the luxury of keeping animals. It seems likely that human association with dogs began when wolves discovered the advantages of lurking around human settlements and were captured as puppies in the wild.

Living with humans, a partly tamed wolf or its offspring would have reacted to danger in the same way it would have if it were in the wild: by fiercely guarding its territory. This was an admirable trait no doubt deeply appreciated by primitive people living in perilous times. This strongly developed defensive instinct was encouraged as the gradual development of the dog took place. These early dogs were all big, powerful animals, wolf-like at first but, as time passed, tending more to the mastiff type we know today.

When man and dog first teamed up to hunt is unclear. Certainly the early Egyptians used them around 8000 years ago; some historians consider that Stone Age man may have had hunting dogs as far back as 10,000 years ago. Man and dog could have first hunted wild boar together then. Interestingly enough, on the wall of a cave in Altamira, Spain, there is an energetic portrait of a boar estimated to have been done 15,000 years before Christ.

Eventually dogs were used to herd animals, taking advantage of a dog's natural instinct to pursue almost anything. They were taught to haul heavily laden sledges in Arctic wastes and to pull small carts in several European countries. Working dogs, with few exceptions, remained big, strong animals. They were intelligent enough to be trained, quite often for complicated tasks.

Among a large group of dogs classified as working dogs are a number used for pig-hunting in this country. They include the German shepherd

(Alsatian), boxer, bull-mastiff, border collie, bearded collie, Dobermann, mastiff, blue heeler, and Rottweiler. Among the terriers are the bull-terrier, Staffordshire bull-terrier, fox-terrier, border terrier, Airedale terrier, and Jack Russell terrier. In the gundog group are the Labrador, German short-haired pointer, and Weimaraner. The hounds include the bloodhound, deerhound, greyhound, whippet, and Rhodesian ridgeback.

Some months after this trip, I had a short holiday with my son, Scott, in Turangi. We went rafting, drove to Taupo one day, mucked about, swam in the motel pool. We hired a couple of horses, too. From Darkie Duff, naturally . . .

'How's it going?'

'Fair enough,' Darkie replied, trying to decide which horse would suit Scott best.

'Been hunting recently?'

'Sure — always find the time for that.' He smiled.

'And . . .?' I pressed him.

He shrugged. 'Y'know . . . few deer, few pigs.'

'Where's my hairy mate?' I asked, not having seen Boofy.

Darkie's face clouded over. 'Like I told you before, he didn't know when to back off a real big 'un.'

'You mean . . .?' I left that hanging there, knowing that his dog was dead.

'Yeah,' was all Darkie Duff said.

Maybe a year later, en route from Auckland to Wellington I thought it would be rather nice to break the tedious drive by taking a break at Turangi, hiring a horse and heading on down to the lakefront. I didn't get to see Darkie Duff that time; he was off in the bush, I was told. Had been there for quite some time, laying low. Out in the bush, then. Living off the land. No problem, of course, for the likes of Darkie Duff.

Top Boar from the Mahia Peninsula

The Mahia Peninsula is a triangular-shaped landmass, quite hilly, that thrusts southwards into the sea from the north-eastern extremity of Hawke Bay. It is twenty-one kilometres long, about twelve kilometres at its widest point, and its highest point, Te Kapu, is 397 metres. The Maori has had a long association with Te Mahia, which means 'indistinct sound', a reference, perhaps, to the ripple of the streams, or the sound of distant birds, or the faraway roar of the surf breaking on sun-drenched Mahia Beach.

It was almost certainly the Maori who introduced pigs to the Mahia Peninsula, possibly by 1840. Given time, some of the descendants of those poorly contained pigs escaped into the adjacent hills, where bracken fern and manuka flourished, where the soil was fertile and the climate agreeable. No one knows for sure when this took place. Over the years the Mahia Peninsula lured Maori and Pakeha pig-hunters alike.

One April day in 1990 four hunters in their twenties — Trevor Lloyd, Keith Ribbon, Tony Stuart and Matthew Bird — set off into the Mahia bush. They took their dogs with them, including Bob, a mastiff/Labrador cross, and Tramp, a mastiff/sheepdog cross. By late afternoon they had been hunting for hours in the rain without success; they hadn't even seen any sign. It was beginning to seem like a complete waste of time.

Then, suddenly, there was a commotion in the heavy bracken fern. Boars were fighting! Maybe they were battling over a sow, maybe over territorial rights. Or they may have just fancied a scrap — a couple of young boars testing each other's prowess, not too serious.

Only Lloyd was armed; he had a .303 rifle and solid-jacketed ammo. They decided that Trevor would sneak in on the combating boars while the others contained the dogs. Unseen, the boars, grunting madly, crunched muscle-packed body against muscle-packed body. This was serious stuff.

Warily, Trevor Lloyd moved into the bracken fern. It was deep, up to the chest of a tall man. There was no way he would be able to see the boars until he was practically upon them. He went on slowly, feeling the excitement building, the palms of his hands slick with sweat as they gripped his ex-military rifle. Again the unseen boars, perhaps wheeling, crashed together. Lloyd's companions waited tensely. They held straining dogs with firm grips, continually hissing at them to keep still, to shut up . . . or else. The dogs knew all about 'or else'.

Suddenly, Trevor Lloyd could see a patch of black hair, more, a vulnerable spot. He raised his rifle, sighted, and a shot rang out. A dull whumping sound, like a gloved fist driven into a solid punching bag.

The dogs were set free. With any luck they would soon catch up with the boar Trevor hadn't fired at. Immediately Bob, the best dog, ran in the opposite direction from where the shot had come. With his super-sharp sense of smell, finely tuned in to pigs, Bob knew something the hunters didn't. Soon he barked, a triumphant sound, the message obvious to dog and pig-hunter alike.

The rest of the dogs streamed past as en masse they ran to link up with Bob. He had winded a black boar near a creek. When the hunters arrived, they saw that the dogs had formed a rough circle around the motionless, glowering animal. He was a boar with a rather nasty look about him, a well-built animal perhaps 230 pounds on the hoof. You couldn't miss his tusks — what a set of hooks!

Where the hell was Trevor? None of the dogs, sensibly, wanted anything to do with the boar. No amount of heated commands could change their minds. Stalemate. All the hunters could do as they stood a little apprehensively behind their dogs was hope that the boar did not break ranks before Trevor arrived in answer to their now frantically yelling voices.

Meantime, Trevor Lloyd was dressing out the boar he had killed, black as the ace of spades, about 100 pounds of well-conditioned meat. Only a four-hour tramp back to where they had left their transport. No problem for fit young types. Suddenly he heard his name being called. He exited the bracken fern at speed. What could top this?

The boar and the dogs were still involved in a Mexican standoff. Had the boar decided to run, he could have easily barrelled his way out, leaving dogs scattered like pins in a bowling alley. Yet for some unknown reason the boar was still there as Trevor Lloyd came running into sight. The boar stood with hackles raised, openly threatening, a promise of mayhem unrealised.

With one glance, Trevor Lloyd took in the situation. He aimed his rifle, yes, steady. The .303 boomed, the noise rolling back and forth over the bracken-clad hills and scrubby gullies of the Mahia Peninsula.

The boar dressed out at 175 pounds. Undrawn, his left and right tusks measured $3^7/_8$ inches and $3^5/_8$ inches respectively. Many a knife has a 4-inch blade; the boar's tusks, well-honed, were no less a weapon. At the base of each tusk the measuring tape stretched to an impressive 2³/₈ inches and it was this thickness, combined with the length and general shape, that made Trevor Lloyd's trophy so outstanding an example of undrawn tusks. They took out top place for undrawn tusks at the NZDA National Trophy Competitions that year.

Big Boars — Big Trouble

How precisely do you define a big boar? Many pig-hunters around the country consider 200 pounds dressed-out to be a 'big boar'. On the hoof, then, we are looking at a minimum weight of around 260 pounds, well on the conservative side. As a comparison, I stand 5 feet 10 inches (1.78 metres) and weigh around 161 pounds. All Black John Kirwan, I believe, tips the scales at around 196 pounds — live weight, naturally. Big John in full flight takes a power of stopping. Add a further 64 pounds to Kirwan and you get an idea of precisely what the smallest of the big boars is all about. Which is not to say that a boar below that mark is of less significance.

The point is, there is always a system to separate the good from the very good and the very good from the excellent, a score to say whether or not a trophy qualifies for the record book. This chapter is mostly about what we shall term 'big boars'.

July 1990: excitement is building steadily for the ninety-five hunters who have entered in the annual three-day competition that is the highlight of the Te Kuiti Pig Hunting Club's calendar. The King Country is the right place to hold a pig-hunting competition. It is, according to the club's secretary, Bob Jeffares, one of the true strongholds of the wild pig in this country. Don't argue with Bob on that point. Significantly, all sows had been excluded from this competition in the previous year, and they had decided to apply the same rules a year later, to assure the future of the sport.

Among those pig-hunters who had been looking forward to the contest in a state of high anticipation was a 45-year-old Otorohanga builder, Wayne Schubert. Wayne, a rangy type well known in these parts for his pig-hunting ability, had been contracted some months previously by Alan Smith, who farmed over at Te Anga, to get rid of some of the pigs ranging the bush country at the back of his farm. While hunting there, Wayne happened to notice the marks of a boar well out of the ordinary, a boar that just might be big enough to win the forthcoming competition. This was a very smart boar, too, because he used younger boars as decoys once the action started, sneaking away to a handy gorge.

About ten days before the competition, Wayne decided to investigate this gorge, to try and pinpoint exactly where the boar had his den. By now his dogs had seen much action. They were fit and hard but always well under control: they broke if and when they were ordered to and they were stockproof, too. Mack was a three-year-old black bull-terrier/whippet cross; Dolly was two years old, a nice brindle colour and the same mixture of breeds as Mack; Nikki was a two-year-old blue heeler cross from across the Tasman; and Stone, at a mere sixteen months, was a brownish bulldog/whippet.

It took time and careful tracking for Wayne to deduce that the boar was almost certainly camped on a small supplejack spur right in the middle of the gorge, which had a total area, he reckoned, of about 41 hectares. The idea now was for the boar to stay there until the competition. But how did you make sure of that? There was a way that almost certainly would work: you baited it with enough food to keep it interested and coming back for more.

Wayne placed his bait out and, more than likely, the boar found it the next night, since he was in the habit of coming to the pasturelands, rooting about, finding the odd dead sheep if he was lucky. He could not have resisted the bait; few protein-hungry pigs would turn up their snouts at the delightful prospect of dining out on goat meat.

The competition opened on a wet Friday: solid, driving rain. But they breed 'em super-tough in the King Country, men with the bark on, like Colin Meads.

Happily, by early afternoon the rain had packed it in. Wondering if the boar had taken the bait, Wayne started with eager steps towards the gorge. His relief was profound — the boar was still coming here to feed overnight. The boar's by now well-beaten track to the gorge was, to Wayne's eyes, distinct. Eagerly the dogs picked up the scent.

The boar was at home on his little supplejack ridge, resting no doubt, his gut full. Tonight he would return to the lovely rank carcasses. Mack found the boar with ease. A sluggish boar that ran for less than forty metres before bailing. He didn't put up a fight. He died there in the gorge, a big black boar that had fed too well.

Elated with his success, for this had been a well-planned hunt perfectly executed, Wayne considered the kill. He was big, all right. Could it be a 200-pounder? It was always difficult to estimate a big boar's weight, easy to be out by twenty or thirty pounds. Wayne, rubbing the back of his neck thoughtfully, wondered if it would be good enough to take the top prize.

Any fears he had were swept away when the competition was over; his

232-pounder easily topped the next heaviest boar, taken by Andrew Todd and Dave Green of Te Anga. Until they saw Wayne's effort hanging on the hook, they'd had every right to feel confident that their 184-pound boar would come out a winner. An amazing twenty-five boars were weighed at this contest, a record that may never be surpassed.

Wayne's prize was $800 worth of flying time with Eastern Bay Trappers Helicopters, a practical gift for a pig-hunter.

In the same July, a 245-pound boar was taken on a property near Waikouaiti, forty-two kilometres north-east of Dunedin. The owner of the run, Stuart Eason, had known for some time that a big pig was ranging the tussocklands on his back block. It was not uncommon to see pigs out there and, as a precaution, he invariably carried a .303 rifle when they were mustering out there.

Indeed, they were mustering the back block when Peter Clulee first saw the boar, bailed by his dogs in a creek. Considering they were huntaways and not pig-dogs, they were doing a fine job. But under no circumstances was he going to do his bit with a pocket-knife! At a gallop, Clulee went to find his boss.

Before Eason shot the rampaging black boar, one of his dogs, Larch, had been badly roughed up, with three broken ribs. Eason, who knew all about the problems pigs could cause at lambing time, was especially glad to have this one out of the way.

Perhaps the most intriguing aspect of pig-hunting is that the actual size of a bailed boar is unknown until that final deadly confrontation.

On a mild but sunny day in November 1990, Larry Wheal and Tom Newell went to the Longwood Forest, a densely timbered region between the lower reaches of the Waiau and Aparima Rivers in Southland. Wild pigs have inhabited the Longwoods far longer than any pig-hunting local can recall and today they range there in low to medium numbers. Wheal and Newell, both in their early forties, were almost as keen to get on the hill as their four dogs: Bully, a five-year-old bull-mastiff cross; four-year-old Bing, another bull-mastiff cross; and three-year-olds Bob, a Staffordshire bull-terrier cross, and Boss, yet another bull-mastiff. The men preferred the strong holding breed because they seldom used a rifle and required a pig to be well contained while one of them delivered the *coup de grâce* with a knife. In the eighteen years they had hunted together, they had shot only three pigs, the biggest of which weighed 220 pounds.

Presently, they were on the last scattered remnants of cultivated land, close to the actual forest. On a previous hunt there, they had found a dead ewe and a pig had been feeding on it. Today they came across a dead lamb, what little was left of it, in much the same general area.

In a big patch of gorse and flax the dogs had bailed a boar. He had typical colouring for the region, black patches on a background of varying shades of brown, running from very light through reddish tones. A furious battle developed. When the boar was done for, only Bob was untouched.

The boar weighed 290 pounds; it goes without saying that this particular animal was the heaviest weighed at the Southern Pig Hunters Club competition.

The lower part of the South Island is renowned not only for the size of its wild boars but also for their fighting qualities; few ever give up without a fight. Only a month before the above-mentioned boar was taken in the Longwoods, another massive animal, with very much the same general colouring, ran out of luck in the Waiau River country. This 289-pounder, with quite exceptional tusks, was accounted for by Peter Broughton, Tony Little, and Steven and Mark Excell. The boar gave as good as he got, goring at least five of the seven dogs involved. One of the dogs ended up in a veterinary hospital.

Darrell Smith of Hawarden, Canterbury, was one of more than fifty hunters who entered an open pig-hunting competition held at Hanmer Springs over Labour Day Weekend 1990. The event started at 1.00 a.m. Saturday and ended 5.00 p.m. Sunday. Smith not only brought in the heaviest boar at 182 pounds, but he also had other boars to keep it company — seven of them. Perhaps he was out to prove something — how good his dogs were, or that his neck of the woods is top pig-hunting country. Reckon Bob Jeffares would have to go along with that.

Meantime, the Mohaka Hotel, on the Napier–Taupo highway, was holding its Labour Day Weekend pig-hunting competition. Taking out first prize in a field of around fifty were Dave Atkinson and Gavin Cottle, whose 249-pound boar was weighed by publican Don Willett. Dave and Gavin shared $750. It wasn't worth it: one of Dave's top dogs was killed and another was so badly spooked by the encounter that it went bush and decided to stay there. These two East Coast hunters are obviously a formidable combination: they took another 200-pound plus boar during 1990 — 216 pounds, to be exact. Yet even that was good enough to take only fifth place in their club's yearly competition.

The last day of May 1991 was fine in the watershed of the Waihou River — more or less at the foot of the Coromandel Peninsula, south of Thames. In the early evening, Lindsay Goudie, a 52-year-old meat grader cum shearer, was pig-hunting on the back of a farm. Previously, he had taken five pigs here — three boars not exceeding 100 pounds and two young sows. They were part of an eleven-strong mob that had been in the habit of raiding the farmer's pastures. First time he had seen them Goudie, a lean six-footer, had shot a boar and sow with his open-sighted .30/30; later, still not using his dog, Patch, he had accounted for two more.

By then the band had split up, he believed. They were now harder to pin down, although mostly they lived in the adjacent pine forest or in a big, gorse-choked gully running back to the pines. They still made forays to root up the farmer's land and quite often came from cover in the late evening. This was the reason Goudie was here today.

A big black boar also ranged pretty much the same territory. In fact, he may have been associated with the mob when the mood took him. The big boar, the farmer had told Goudie, had been sighted on his land two or three times, once by his brother, who had come across two boars resting in thick cover. Fortunately for the big boar, the brother had shot his much smaller companion and, despite reloading quickly, had no opportunity to shoot the other one.

On this particular evening Goudie, who actually enjoyed hunting without a dog, had decided to give Patch a run. She was a $2^1/_2$-year-old bull-terrier/cattle-dog cross, a sensible sort of dog, not given to undue excitement. Around mid-evening a cold wind picked up, although it was still fine. By then, man and dog had worked across the farmer's paddocks to come to the gorse-filled gully. On the broken rim of the gully, Goudie paused, the muzzle of his Winchester pointing towards the ground, his thumb curled around the hammer.

Slowly, Goudie scanned left to right across and into the gully so that, in one searching sweep, he saw all of it. Patch stood by her master's side, scenting. There was no sign of pigs. Hmm . . . He decided to wait for a while and, with his rifle across his drawn up knees, he sat out of the wind.

Patch looked at Goudie. Goudie looked at Patch. Patch took a tentative step and Goudie, with a smile, motioned with his hand. Patch started down the gully. The hunter watched with interest as his brown-and-white pig-dog started up the far side of the gully, homing in on the pines.

Then it happened. Upwind of Patch, a large black-coated animal pushed its way out of a tight mixture of manuka and gorse and stood there, almost arrogantly, in the open. Goudie, still sitting, drew a sharp breath. This had to be the boar the farmer had told him about.

The boar scented the dog curiously; he had never been hunted by dogs. Goudie worked the Winchester's silky-smooth action and eased, with hardly a sound, a 150-grain Winchester Silvertip expanding bullet into the breach. The boar still stood there, transfixed. Just as carefully, Goudie closed the action, then brought back the knurled hammer to full cock with a barely audible click-click.

Swivelling his hips on the ground, the better to aim, Goudie squinted down the short barrel, aligning the front sight with the rear one. Everything blurred except for the narrow blade of the rifle and the boar's solid shoulder padding. The recoil of the .30/30 was severe enough for the hunter to notice; the report was loud but lacking real echo. Instantly, the boar was running into the gully. But already he was losing momentum, starting to falter, about to tumble, then falling heavily, crashing head over heels into the thicket.

The big black boar, to Lindsay Goudie's deep and lasting satisfaction, dressed out at 218½ pounds. Equally rewarding was the fact that it proved to be the outstanding boar taken by a member of the Coromandel Pig Hunting Club in 1991. All up, members of this particular club took seventy-one boars weighing 100 pounds or more during 1991, in country no great distance from New Zealand's largest city.

Mountain Man

Right from the very early days of pre-European settlement, domestic and semi-wild pigs, hearing the irresistible call of freedom, escaped from Maori settlements or camps, where they were mostly poorly contained, and soon reverted to feral animals. In the process, perhaps because of their close contact with humans, they became potentially more dangerous and certainly more elusive than if they had been born wild.

Later, after the Pakeha had opened up the hinterland and farms scarred the fringes of civilisation, some of his pigs, for precisely the same reason, vanished into the adjacent forested country. Whether or not they were distinctly Hampshire, Berkshire or Tamworth stock made no difference; somehow, they had pricked up their large ears to a distant call and had responded to it, casting aside all pretence of domesticity.

Wild pigs!

In the cool, overcast late afternoon of a September day Brett Millward arrived home after spending a day searching unsuccessfully for pigs on Pirongia Mountain, south-west of Hamilton. Pigs were in medium numbers there then, and it was rare for him to miss out.

Brett and Steve Millward's 250-hectare farm, on which they ran sheep, cattle and sometimes pigs, was bounded on two sides by native bush, Maori land on one side and reserve on the other. The reserve was a tiny part of the 14,262-hectare Pirongia State Forest Park, which here in Raglan County had a self-contained section dominated by the 755-metre Karioi Mountain. Steeped in history, Karioi Mountain is approximately 30 kilometres north-west of the better-known and certainly more visible Pirongia Mountain (962 metres) and its densely forested western buttresses, often quite steep, form the coastal landmass known as Woody Head.

In the first month of spring 1985, a most elusive wild boar ranged

Karioi Mountain. He had done so for at least twelve years. He was known by some as the 'Phantom Pig of Karioi Mountain' and by others as 'Mountain Man'. To Brett Millward, a 28-year-old married man with three young children, Mountain Man was something of an obsession. He and Mountain Man went back a long way.

By and large, Mountain Man's origins were rather obscure. What is certain, however, is that he and another pig had escaped from some itinerant people who in the late 1960s or early 1970s had camped near the bush on the coastal side of Karioi Mountain. Mountain Man was of Tamworth stock, that is, he was off-white. Of all domestic pigs, the Tamworth is believed to revert more quickly to a feral state than any other. His companion was black, like the pigs that roamed Pirongia Mountain. The black animal was also a barrow, unable to breed. Both pigs were about five to six months old when they escaped and both, it is believed, were already half wild. They soon became fully wild.

In 1973 the Millward family came from the Taranaki backblocks to farm in Raglan County. This was bad luck for the black barrow, because that very year, while returning to fresh pig sign that had been found in rough country on the back of the farm, Steve Millward's dogs bailed it up. A single shot from Steve's .30/30 Winchester ended the barrow's short life. Later Steve said to his brother, Brett, that unless he was very much mistaken he had heard another pig sneaking away.

Like it or not, Mountain Man was on his own on Karioi Mountain. As he grew older all signs that he had once been domesticated fled like 'roos before a bushfire. His once off-white coat turned a dark tawny shade. Naturally enough, he grew tusks far bigger than those of any domestic pig; they were tremendous fighting weapons. Soon there was not the slightest hint of a kink in his tail; it was as straight as an arrow.

As with all true wild boars, he developed a body shield, which, in most animals, is only about the shoulders. Not so with Mountain Man: his body shield, a thick layer of tough skin, covered the neck, shoulders, chest, flanks and even his underparts. In effect, he was armour-plated, priceless and essential protection should he combat a rival boar, a tusk-slashing, teeth-raking creature with mayhem uppermost on his blood-crazed mind. Adult boars killed by hunters are frequently criss-crossed with tell-tale scars. They are seldom deep enough to cause real injury and at best may be described as superficial wounds.

So Mountain Man was well equipped for battle. The trouble was that there were no boars for him to fight it out with, and no sows to mate with, either. Perhaps Mountain Man's isolation, which continued for at least four years, dictated his future. He would display the strong traits of a true loner and it is possible that because of the circumstances he lost his sex drive; or perhaps he never really knew this feeling. Certainly he made no attempt to mate with sows on farms adjacent to the mountain. The boar's testicles shrunk or never really developed fully. Whatever. He also lacked that rank, peculiar, sexual odour adult wild boars often have about them; he was not ejaculating on his belly hairs as a male goat, bull thar or rampant red deer stag will.

By early 1976, when he was perhaps six years old, he was in his prime. Given a generous measure of good fortune, he could live to about twenty years of age. Perhaps by now he had gained his full weight; that, of course, could fluctuate quite dramatically according to the food supply. In all probability in the late summer of 1976 he weighed 300 pounds on the hoof. It was mostly hard-packed muscle.

During 1977 two sows and a boar, all captured on Pirongia Mountain, were liberated on Karioi Mountain. Pigs on Pirongia at this time were all black, with, in some cases, white feet. (More recently, black-and-white pigs have been taken there and possibly other variations as well.)

Towards the end of the decade, the occasional person began to see the spoor of what was obviously a huge boar on Karioi Mountain. It was generally believed that this animal was the off-white, Tamworth-like pig that had escaped years ago. Perhaps because the black pig had been a barrow it was presumed the white one had been cut too.

A further liberation of nine pigs, including three pregnant sows, was made on Karioi Mountain in 1980. Again they came from Pirongia Mountain.

In November 1980 Forest Service hunters Peter Hill and John Roberts were working on wild goat control on Karioi Mountain. Because of the difficult terrain, and also because many goats become surprisingly cunning if hunted regularly, they had little option but to use dogs. Pete's dogs were a cattle-dog called Ben and Scott, a corgi cross. John's hunting companion was a black Labrador cross called Bo, which he'd found in the Hamilton pound.

One afternoon Pete was hunting a heavily bushed gorge, where he observed three white goats poised in profile on a high, sharp-backed spur. Using a Remington Model 600 .222, he shot two of them. Even before the shooting was over, Ben had vanished. Tailing his kills, Pete presumed he had taken off after the lone survivor. Pete shrugged; Ben would turn up again, he always did. It was more likely Pete would find him out on the farmlands where, a few hours ago, he'd left his trailbike.

Four hours later, Pete found a very subdued Ben lying next to his bike. He was shocked to discover that Ben had been badly ripped in the shoulder. No wild goat — no matter how sharp-tipped his horns — could have possibly caused that. A boar was undoubtedly responsible. But there were no pigs on Karioi Mountain, were there?

Pete and John made enquiries, and heard the story of how a white barrow had taken to the mountain in the early 1970s. Interestingly enough, no mention was made of the pig liberation of 1977, or the more recent one. There were some things you didn't tell Forest Service employees.

Fired up now with the idea of catching this barrow, Pete and John covered most of the mountain. They found fresh rooting, consistent with a large male. Later Bo, ranging ahead of his master, came face to face with the real thing. When he rejoined John, he'd acquired a deep gash under his right front leg, snaking across his ribs.

When I talked with both men in January 1981, they still hadn't seen the pig responsible for ripping two of their dogs. It is, of course, possible that another boar, and not Mountain Man, gored their dogs. I would like to think that Mountain Man was the boar in question; perhaps you feel that way too.

By 1982 pig numbers on Karioi Mountain had grown considerably, as a result of the 1980 liberation rather than the earlier one. Soon, pig rooting was a common sight on pasturelands. The news that good pig-hunting could be had on Karioi Mountain lured many hunters there, most of whom had heard of Mountain Man. For it was about now that the name stuck with the tawny-coloured boar that, locals reckoned, had a hoofmark you could liken to that of a yearling steer.

All hunters who came into contact with Mountain Man agreed that he ranged high, the steeper the better. He was constantly on the move, with regular beats in both the forest park and adjacent Maori land. Mountain Man's distinct spoor was observed by Brett Millward on hunting trips and when he went trapping possums over the winter. Another possum trapper, Terry Nolan, was also keen to account for Mountain Man, by now a common topic of conversation in Raglan hotels. Once Nolan saw a full-grown nikau that had been uprooted by the great boar. Commercial fisherman Wayne Robbs was another hunter who had Mountain Man on his mind. His dogs once tracked the boar from one side of the mountain, clear over the top of it, to the far side and then lost it.

The quest to take out Mountain Man grew in intensity during 1983 and 1984. At least six dogs were killed, and numerous dogs were badly ripped. Mountain Man had become a legend in his own time.

One September evening in 1985 Brett Millward arrived back at the farm from Pirongia Mountain, had a quick cup of tea, and went to feed his dogs. He decided to check some dead sheep in his back paddock. With his ten-year-old bull-terrier Scotty, Millward set off, after telling his wife, Suzanne, of his intentions.

The compact Millward, with a Marlin .44 Magnum in the crook of his arm, walked quickly to the back paddock. To his surprise there were no ewes or lambs in sight. Had something frightened them? Scotty? Millward's eyes darted every which way — there was no sign of Scotty. A name suddenly hammered urgently in Millward's mind. Mountain Man.

Swiftly, Millward followed a small stream that ran along the fringe of the grazing land. It took him to a place where, he knew, Mountain Man had a regular beat. Stock still, he stared at the ground; there were huge tracks, as fresh as morning dew.

Millward took a deep, steadying breath and ——

Scotty barked!

Where? Millward's eyes darted to a low saddle — he was sure Scotty was on the far side of it, down in a scrubby little gully. Scotty barked again and Millward lunged into a hard, driving run.

Topping the saddle, he gulped air deep into his already tortured lungs. Scotty barked. With the spot pinpointed, Millward raced downslope, the boar's angry, deep-toned rumbling rising ominously to him. It had to be Mountain Man.

Millward was right: Scotty had bailed the great tawny-coated boar. Now, with the ability to hold as well as find and bail, Scotty moved in closer to the boar. Mountain Man, despite his prodigious size, moved like lightning. Whump! Scotty sailed high in the air. Then, with a breathless Millward only a few paces away, the courageous dog picked himself up and immediately went back to confront the boar. Again Scotty had the wind driven from his lungs as Mountain Man, wheeling, smashed him to the ground. Mountain Man broke free of cover.

What a monster! thought Millward. At a range of about 25 metres, he fired; a 240-grain projectile struck the boar high up behind the ribs, mushrooming, breaking the spinal column. Mountain Man went down hard, roaring in pain. In went Scotty. But the boar was far from finished. He would fight until the bitter end. He whipped his great head back and forth, slashed open Scotty's throat and hurled him at least two metres. Groggily Scotty started to crawl away, dragging himself like a gutshot beast to cover.

Far from composed, Millward fired again, a head shot. It was all over. Adrenalin pumping crazily, he stared at the fallen boar in awe. It seemed inconceivable to him that the great tawny-coated boar that had ranged Karioi Mountain since the early 1970s was no more, blown away like a puff of smoke on a windy day.

Scotty whimpered.

Millward, his brief reverie over, rushed to his dog's side. 'Hey, fella.' His voice shook.

Apart from the deep gash to Scotty's throat, he was also gored in the chest. Looks bad, Millward thought, real bad. And yet, he reassured himself, he had seen dogs hurt far worse than this survive. He had to get him to the vet in Raglan as quickly as possible.

Scotty made a fine recovery, thanks to the expert attention of Ross Loveridge. Scotty lived, as they say, to fight another day and finally died of old age. No brave-hearted pig-dog could wish for more than that.

Brett Millward found that Mountain Man was unmarked by man or dog, which put paid to one hunter's claim that he had wounded him. Incredibly, his body shield was 2½ to 3 inches thick at the shoulder. Dressed-out, he weighed a lean 287 pounds; Millward believes he could have weighed

Jack Russell terrier, at their best in heavy cover.

Russell Bryant's bull-terrier cross has proved to be an ideal pig-dog.

Waco.

Ken Johnson and his Appaloosa, Trinity.

Kunekune pig.

Winchester Model 1894, a lever-action rifle, like the ones used in cowboy movies.

Ruger Mini-14, calibre .223.

From left: Sako Finnwolf .308 with Marlin .44 Magnum; Marlin 1895, firing the potent .444 Marlin cartridge; and Ruger All-weather Model 77 Mark II, ideal for open-country hunting.

a good 100 pounds more had he been fat. He is also convinced that Mountain Man did not breed with any of the sows that were liberated on Karioi Mountain and that he was perhaps as close to a barrow as you can get.

Today the head of Mountain Man, mounted by Owen Reed of Stratford, has pride of place in the lounge of Brett Millward's home. Invariably it is a talking point when people drop in; but then, the feats of the legendary Mountain Man will long be a topic of conversation in Raglan County.

Waco

Five-year-old Waco had bailed the black boar high in a rough creek, known as Stoney, on the western side of the Pisa Range. His deep-toned barking held some urgency and it carried far.

Before he was disturbed, the boar had been devouring the starchy roots of a big clump of speargrass. Understandably, he wasn't too kindly disposed towards the strongly built Weimaraner. Fact is, he was downright fractious! But the chase, in and out of several scrub-choked gullies nudging the retreating snow line, had him huffing and puffing like an old-time steamroller making hard work of it on a steep country road. With hackles raised the glowering boar was, for the moment, prepared to stand his ground while regaining his breath and, perhaps, composure.

Waco, panting, considered the boar with a thoughtful expression on his intelligent face. It is interesting to note that of all the recognised gundogs — setters, English pointers, pointer-retrievers, retrievers and spaniels — only the Weimaraner is used to hunt pigs in this country. Of course, many 'Labradors' are used here, but they are invariably crossed with another breed — bull-terrier, for instance — to produce something far tougher than your run-of-the-mill Labrador, which is something of a softie. For the record, the Weimaraner breed originated at Weimar, Germany, around the beginning of the last century. It has a generous dollop of red schweisshund blood to produce a dog for all seasons, one that can point, retrieve and trail.

True to form, Waco began to use diversionary tactics to harass the boar. He frequently cast a pale eye towards a clear-cut ridge. Any moment now he expected the rest of the team to arrive, although not many were on duty today. Just one, in fact — his beloved master, who, in dicey situations like this, often appeared just in the nick of time, like the Lone Ranger.

Ken Johnson, with long, Levi's-clad legs wrapped around a roping saddle, and familiar excitement welling up, cut up a sharp slope, topped a ridge, and rapidly checked his heaving mount. His eyes narrowed and he sucked in his breath sharply: he was looking at the biggest boar he had ever seen on the Pisa Range. A good 200 pounds, he reckoned. Held on a too-tight rein, Trinity snorted apprehensively; the six-year-old Appaloosa gelding was invariably spooky around wild pigs.

'Ease up there!' Ken's voice was firm.

Still Trinity was inclined to fidget.

Aware of a new and even more ominous threat, the boar suddenly began to run pell-mell between clumps of thorn-armed matagouri. Waco needed no urging and tried, but failed, to grab hold of a back leg. Boar and dog vanished and the lanky Johnson removed a gloved hand from the well-worn butt of his Winchester '94. Trinity responded to the light pressure on her flanks; the tracks of both boar and dog were clear in the overnight snow.

Born in Minnesota, USA, Ken Johnson arrived in New Zealand via Australia in 1972. A builder by profession, the 22-year-old found work easily enough. In Wanaka, he met a Wellingtonian called Val, who shared his love of the outdoors, particularly horses. Together, a good-looking couple, they went horse trekking. They eventually married and purchased a small, rundown place out in the Cardrona Valley, twenty minutes' drive from Wanaka.

It turned out to be a fine place to raise kids and horses: two boys, two girls and lots of horses, particularly the quiet yet spirited Appaloosa breed. They started a horse-trekking business and it went well. A keen hunter from way back, Ken, who had first hunted pigs in outback New South Wales, was thrilled to learn there were pigs on the Pisa Range. Wild pork often featured on the menu at the Johnsons' spread in the Cardrona Valley.

On this particular day in late winter, roast pork was not on Ken's mind as Waco's deep-gutted woofing told him that the boar was bailed up like the passengers of a Cobb & Co. stagecoach confronted by bushrangers. The boar whipped back his head and swung left and right as the Weimaraner, as elusive as a grey ghost, side-stepped. Waco snarled. He had detested pigs since his first hunt: the hunting tradition was bred deeply in him and, had he been born in his homeland, he would have tackled red stags with eagerness too. While short of trophy size, the boar's tusks were formidable weapons. Just one slashing cut across Waco's taut stomach would reveal what he'd had for breakfast.

Nearby, Ken dismounted with urgency, slipped the reins through a wire fence and secured them. The lever-action rifle Ken had yanked from its scabbard was in keeping with his cowboy image: screen cowboys invariably carried Winchesters — either Model '92 or '94 — even if the movie was set in the 1880s! As he stepped over the top wire of the fence, Ken Johnson caught sight of the black boar for a second time.

Something primitive burned like live coals in the boar's eyes as Waco, no lightweight at 50 pounds, went in fast and slammed into the boar's rear end. Spinning like a slowing top, the boar was again unable to make contact with the elusive creature that by this stage had driven it near demented with rage.

Ken, with his rifle fully cocked, knew that he had to end it quickly, otherwise ——

'Waco!' Ken's voice cracked with the authority of a 10-foot bullwhip.

Waco moved a safe distance from the boar. The .30/30 bucked and a Winchester Power-Point cartridge went deep into the boar's body, burning a channel through solid muscle, smashing bone, and ending a life. Automatically, Ken reloaded, although he knew that it wasn't necessary to shoot again. More than one pig-hunter, perhaps wanting to save a bullet, has paid the sickening price of wounded or dead dogs because he assumed a hard-hit boar was dead meat. The .30/30 roared again.

Presently, Ken gathered up the reins and mounted; he would return with a packhorse to take the dressed-out carcass home. The wind whipped in from the south and he narrowed his eyes against its icy blast; snowflakes flurried. No matter — Ken was savouring the deep satisfaction of making the kill; for now, that was more than enough.

It was towards the end of winter 1990. The sky was the colour of beaten lead and snowflakes drifted down. State Highway 89, the unsealed road linking Queenstown and Alexandra, was not the sort of back-country route you'd take for a pleasant Sunday drive. Thunk! Thunk! Thunk! The windscreen wipers were working overtime. Loose metal crunched under grinding tyres.

Concentrating hard on the road, ahead of me I saw a late-model car, hauling a wildly swaying caravan, lurch around a particularly nasty hairpin corner. I could've sworn I'd seen a Works sign stating caravans were forbidden on the highway. Hogging the road, the car and caravan went past me. There were a couple of kids in the caravan; they waved to me. Wasn't getting any better, was it?

Soon I was probing deep into the valley of the Cardrona River, which was just a stream this high up. With the snow and the mist I might have been in the Scottish highlands, although there were no shaggy-coated highland cattle, just some merino sheep on the grassy hillfaces, a dead rabbit on the road and a damp-looking harrier hawk sitting on a fencepost.

Eventually I reached my destination — Ken and Val Johnson's place.

'Coffee? Tea?' Val asked in their comfy kitchen cum living room.

Ken was straddling a chair, facing a small potbellied stove that was chucking out the heat. He had just finished telling me, in laconic style, about the big black boar he and Waco had taken a few years ago.

'Still got the thirty-thirty?' I asked.

'Nope,' Ken replied, shaking his head.

He explained that he now regretted letting it go. But, like many hunters

— whatever the game they were after — he'd enjoyed experimenting with the .30/30 and various makes of firearms and different calibres. The fact was, it didn't matter what you clobbered them with but where.

Nevertheless, Ken Johnson's firearms tended to be of a certain type. It was to be expected: basically, he was a horseman who also happened to hunt pigs, so he had no use for a heavy, long-barrelled rifle. What he needed was a compact, lightweight tool that fitted easily into a saddle scabbard and could be carried slung without much difficulty. It turned out Ken's latest pet was a far cry from the successful Winchester models 1892 and 1894 (the 1892 was very widely used for pig-hunting in the 1920s and 1930s). His new weapon was as modern as they came: a Ruger Mini-14 Ranch Rifle with a stainless-steel barrel and calibre of .223; it was a five-shot auto-loader of time-proven design.

'Pigs?'

'No problems,' Ken replied. He handed me the nifty $6^1/_2$-pound Ruger complete with a 1 x 75-4.5 Bushnell Banner scope.

I hadn't really expected him to have any trouble dealing with a pig at close range with a .223. After all, a 55-grain slug behind the ear will do the job just as effectively as a projectile three times that weight. The shoulder area is, of course, another story.

I must admit I had, until quite recently, loathed any sort of firearm with a stainless-steel barrel. Really, it was much too radical, too G.I. Joe for someone who grew up on movies like *Winchester '73*, *High Noon* and, best of all, *Shane*. I preferred the butt-end of a long arm to come from a deep groove of walnut trees and when I purchased a rifle I expected it to have a good coating of blue over all of the metal parts.

Times change. Until a few years ago I hadn't hunted on Stewart Island or, for that matter, carried a rifle on the south-west coast of Fiordland. Both experiences are apt to change anyone's line of thinking. Both of these places are so damp that the sandflies are born with rheumatism and the red deer have been known to invest in a good raincoat. Swanndris are too heavy for them when wet, and they tend to favour camouflage designs, which perhaps explains why you can spend a helluva lot of time in that sodden part of the country and still not see anything sporting a red (in summer) or grey (in winter) coat. Certainly my Sako rifle was not at all impressed with the wet, salty, metal-rusting conditions.

A rifle with a stainless-steel barrel and a synthetic stock is well nigh perfect for water-logged hunting conditions with, in both Stewart Island and Fiordland, a surprising amount of humidity. It seems to me that many a pig-hunter will turn to a compact firearm better able to cope with wet conditions. The rather limited choice of the present time will no doubt broaden as more and more riflemen see the obvious advantages.

Some think a stainless-steel barrel is too shiny, a dead giveaway in sika or whitetail territory. But 'camo' tape wound tightly around the barrel fixes that. Main thing is, though, a shiny barrel need not concern the pig-hunter:

pigs have notoriously poor eyesight. I can vouch for that — on several photographic expeditions, with the wind in my favour, I have been able to sneak in and get very close.

Pigs are much more active and far-ranging in winter, and as a result are likely to turn up on or near cultivated land and pig-hunters, well aware of this, are normally more active, too. Winter — naturally enough — is often wet, which means pig-hunters pursue their dogs through all types of rubbish when the weather is far from inspiring. Soaking fern, bracken, manuka or, worse, clumps of interlocked matagouri can ruin the stock of a brand-new rifle in no time. Also not helpful to maintaining a rifle in tip-top condition is a sudden dunking in a raging stream or, for that matter, a metal-clanging descent down a rocky face.

So a hunting rifle does take a fair hammering, and never more than when the name of the game is pigs. When that final confrontation takes place, as it does week in, week out in New Zealand, then quite often that Winchester '94 or Marlin '95 is 'blooded' in more ways than one.

Seems to me that's pretty traditional, too.

There were encouraging breaks in the cloud when I left Ken Johnson tending to one of his fine Appaloosa horses, hipshot at a hitching rail. Big, light-coloured Waco, squatting on his ample rump, watched me walk to my vehicle.

'See ya, Ken!'

'So long, buddy!'

Waco showed his fine teeth. I presume he was smiling.

From the Johnsons' place it is a slow and gradual climb to a low saddle on State Highway 89 that forms part of the upper watershed of the Cardrona River. Beyond there — in case you're interested — the road drops torturously to link up with State Highway 6 a few kilometres out of Queenstown.

Before I reached the saddle, I pulled to a halt. I got out of the car; it was cold, all right. I gathered my Driza-Bone about me. Yes, this little gully just off the road looked like the spot Val Johnson had described to me. A couple of summers ago the Johnsons were returning home along this same route. Imagine their surprise when, in this little gully, they observed a mob of pigs feeding with relish on the soft, yellowing fruit of a number of low-growing gooseberry bushes.

'You know what,' Ken had said, picking up the story. 'My goddam rifle was back at home!'

Make Mine a Marlin

On the first day of spring in 1987, we came down from matagouri and tussock covered slopes to a scrubby-coated bench above the winding Waimakariri. It had been a good hunt, full of interest, and the young animal Winston McGregor had taken for meat was in its prime. There was no TB here — you could bet on that.

Winston, Kevin Whitelaw, Harvey Taylor and I were grouped together. We talked over the hunt, easy with each other, as the dogs lay in the sun. I looked over Kevin's rifle. It was out of the famed Sako stable — the Finnwolf model. It is a strong name, bringing to mind a vivid image of an icy forest in Finland and near-starving wolves moving through a silent, snow-locked world. To the best of my knowledge, the Finnwolf was Sako's only entry into the US-dominated lever-action field. It was not entirely successful, mainly because it was prone to problems with feeding cartridges from magazine to breach, and Sako finally discontinued it. Kevin, too, had been frustrated with the cartridge jamming in the magazine. Still, the Finnwolf is a nice-looking piece, which, after all, is what you'd expect of any firearm bearing the name Sako. Today it's a much sought-after rifle, a collector's piece. It is a bit heavy for general pig-hunting, though, and is used as a compromise firearm for pig-hunters who often hunt other game, too.

While the boys chatted amongst themselves, I put down the Sako and picked up Winston's rifle or, to be more accurate, carbine. Now this was my idea of a pig-hunting smokepole: a Marlin Model 1894, not an original, you understand, but one made much more recently but still bearing that famous date tag.

With its short barrel, Winston's Marlin was chambered for real potent pig medicine: .44 Magnum. You can't really go wrong with the .44 Magnum for bustin' pigs in thick cover, particularly when using the 240-grain projectile at a muzzle velocity of 1760 fps. The .44 Magnum cartridge is a major step up from the .44/40 Winchester round, which was used extensively in this country when wild pigs were truly rampant in the 1920s and 1930s. In recent times, many local pig-hunters have realised the advantages of the .44 Magnum on pigs. Like Winston McGregor and Brett Millward, a fair number of them handle a Marlin 1894, too. Short-barrelled, lightweight, quick-handling, amply powerful . . . why not?

Another Marlin rifle that has found popularity with pig-hunters is also based on a famous model of a distant age: the Model 1895. Called Marlin's Big Gun, it could be obtained in the mid 1890s in calibres of .45/70, .45/90 and .40/82. The introduction of other powerful cartridges would come later. Like the Model 1894, it was discontinued in 1917. Marlin reintroduced the Model 1895 in 1972 with a calibre of .45/70. New Zealand pig-hunters who carry today's version of Marlin's Big Gun fire an entirely different calibre from those originally used by the Model 1895 — the .444 Marlin. Using a 240-grain projectile, and with a muzzle velocity of 2400 fps, the range and killing power far exceeds that of the less ambitious .44 Magnum load.

Suddenly I was aware of a slight pressure against my leg. It was Flynn, the young, good-natured son of twelve-year-old Ben, a handsome beardie sheepdog. The third of Winston's dogs, Fred, a brown-and-white animal, was a rather pleasing mixture, according to his amiable master, of kelpie, Labrador and cattle-dog.

'How's Flynn?' I asked him.

Flynn showed his teeth, batted his tail. Flynn was obviously OK. I dropped to one knee to pat him and Fred ambled over for some attention, too. Top dogs, the very best of dogs where Winston McGregor was concerned.

'Better get moving, eh?' Kevin said.

'Yeah,' agreed Harvey.

With a grunt, Winston hoisted the pig's carcass onto his back.

'Carry my rifle, Phil?' Winston said.

I was only too pleased to.

In single file, men and dogs started down to the Waimakariri River. One of the men carried a Marlin rifle; one of the dogs, Flynn, would soon be killed by a boar. What was new in the continuing saga of hunters and wild pigs in New Zealand?

Nothing Like a Mud Bath

A steady drizzle was falling this May 1987 morning, and a leaden sky gave no indication things were about to change. Ahead of me were three other horsemen. John Williamson, thirty-five, farmed at Paparangi station, some 43 kilometres north-west of Wanganui; Graham Palamountain, twenty-eight, was self-employed and lived in Wanganui; and Mike Davie was a taxi driver in Wellington. With lunging motions, our horses, in single file, topped a grassy ridge, the end of a sudden climb up from the Mangapurua Stream, in the watershed of the Wanganui River. Now they stood close together, stirrup to stirrup. John was mounted on Rod, a strongly built gelding; Graham was lucky enough to be riding a lovely blue roan called Free; and Mike was astride a chunky station hack called Brownie that, considering he was a real novice at this caper, was doing remarkably well.

The effort of reaching this spot had been considerable and we lingered while the horses caught their breath. Their coats were dark with sweat and steam, which could have been mistaken for mist, lifted from their overheated bodies into the chilly air. I fingered Bay's thick mane. He was a good-natured animal, easy to get along with and good to ride, an honest toiler just like the other horses. Like the dogs they gave their all and asked for very little in return.

We went on, the dogs trotting enthusiastically ahead. There were seven of them. I have yet to meet a pig-dog that isn't a character and Butch, Smoko, Sue, Patch, Sparky, Tike and Chippy were not exceptions. Soon we came to a saucer-like basin, mostly flanked by ponga trees. There were the remnants of a fenceline here, a reminder that once, optimistic people had lived here. They were farmer settlers, back in the old days. The last family had departed the beautiful, 30-kilometre valley in 1944.

Now the valley belonged to the pigs and a mushrooming feral goat population. We had observed antler marks on a few bushes and trees on a spine-like ridge: the tell-tale signs that a red deer stag or, more likely, a fallow deer buck, had somehow found its way into the valley. But it was pigs that had brought me here and there was plenty in this basin to interest me. Fresh rooting scarred the bright green grass and there was a channel-like wallow created by, and for, the pigs.

We dismounted. With the heavy reins looped casually around his left forearm, John, a rangy six-footer with a quiet air of menace about him, cast a dark eye at the rooting.

'Buggers were here last night, eh?' he said to Graham, his long-time hunting companion.

Graham, strongly built, nodded in agreement. 'Say so.'

John reached into a pocket in his red-and-black Swanndri and fished out a packet of tobacco. With a wry expression, Mike massaged his saddle-pounded backside; John, noticing it, grinned like a grey nurse shark spotting two whitish legs dangling invitingly above.

'You're doin' OK, Mike,' John said, making no attempt to hide a big grin.

Mike's reply was an expressive grunt.

Letting Free crop at the grass, Graham angled across to the nearest patch of rooting. There was a Winchester '94 slung across his shoulder and it looked so natural that it occurred to me that he might have been given it, instead of a cuddly teddy bear, when he was a real young fella. Securing my horse to a low bush, I went to the wallow. Obviously it was in regular use — the local version of a beauty parlour.

'Hey!' Graham called from over at the rooting. 'A boar was here recently.'

'Uh-huh.' John was matter-of-fact.

Back in the Urewera country I had come across many such wallows used by either pig or deer but not, I suspect, by both.

John said, 'Boar was here, too.'

The hoofmarks showed up clearly in the slush surrounds of the wallow. Still, it was to be expected: a boar will have several wallows in his territory providing, of course, the nature of the country lends itself to it. A pig's skin is thick, and an adult boar's is especially thick. Since a pig does not possess sweat glands, the act of wallowing helps to keep it cool, and a thick layer of dried mud is marvellous protection against biting insects and assorted parasites.

Near this particular wallow in the Mangapurua Valley there was a rough-barked ponga, the lower part of which was used by pigs to rub dried mud off their shoulders and backs and thus rid themselves of ticks or whatever else may cause them marked distress. This rubbing motion, carried out with brisk movements and much grunting, also toughens the skin again after the softening-up caused by a lengthy mud bath. By looking closely at such trees, it is sometimes possible to observe tusk marks on the bark. They may mean nothing to you or me, and almost certainly sows and young stuff ignore the message, but they warn off potential rivals.

Since elephants, rhinoceroses, deer, warthogs and, of course, wild and domestic pigs (given the opportunity) wallow all year round, it is clear that it not only cools their overheated bodies and helps rid them of parasites, but is also a highly pleasurable experience.

Presently, we mounted up. The drizzle was still there; the sky was even darker. The well-sheltered basin was behind us now. Since the mid 1940s, and possibly earlier, very few humans would have been there and those that did, I expect, would not have lingered long. Essentially it was the realm of wild pigs, about as remote as you can get in this country. Over the years generations of pigs would have used this and other such wallows in the valley. Soon, perhaps overnight, a boar would return here. He would immerse himself in the glutinous mixture much as you and I lower ourselves into a hot tub after a long day on the ski slopes. Later, when the mud had dried, he would move to the ponga. When his toilet was complete, he would be clean; he was by instinct a clean animal.

Maurice and Robert Burton tell a lovely little story about wallowing in *The Animal World*:

> A party of tourists was assembled in a hide, in the Infolosi Park in southern Africa. They were watching a warthog sow and her two piglets wallowing. Finally, the sow emerged from the wallow completely covered in mud, followed by her two piglets, one of which was well caked all over with mud and the other of which was muddy except on the back. The trio had not proceeded far when the sow looked at her offspring with the clean back and then nudged it towards the wallow and drove it in again. The sow also entered the wallow and rolled in the mud once again, but on her back, as if trying to indicate to the piglet that this was what it should do. After a while the piglet appeared to have got the message, turned on its back and wallowed, whereupon the sow got to her feet and walked out of the wallow with her youngsters following her.
>
> The tourists were highly amused and gave vent to a chorus of laughter. . . . People often talk glibly about an animal teaching its young, but concrete examples of this are hard to come by, so much so that some ethologists declare that an animal never actively teaches its young, but merely educates it by example. There may be some truth in this, but to the assembled tourists the scene they witnessed was a clear-cut case of animal education.

To Lose a Good Mate

Somehow, wild pigs and the Wanganui River backblocks go hand in hand, each synonymous with the other. Wild pigs were well entrenched here by the time the first European settlers moved in with wonderful dreams, never to be realised. Since then, untold Europeans have run farms and stations in this rugged part of the North Island; like the local Maori, to whom the wild pig is still an integral part of life, few if any would have been untouched by the antics of this most resourceful of wild creatures.

Traditionally, wild pigs are black in this part of New Zealand. They are fine pigs, often, in the case of mature boars, wonderfully streamlined animals. One such boar had become something of a fixation with well-known hunter Bob Pittaway. Bob had seen the boar, which he called 'Grandad', several times before he finally got it. Not wanting to steal Bob's thunder, for he may well write Grandad's story himself one day, I will only say that the dressed-out boar weighed 275 pounds and measured nearly seven feet, and that it was the biggest boar taken in the Wanganui River backblocks for quite some time.

Mangapurua station is on the western side, and in the upper reaches, of the Wanganui River. It is situated more or less directly opposite Jerusalem, and is, in fact, closer to Raetihi than Wanganui. The station has been owned by Hans and Shereen Brink since 1984.

In the winters after they bought the property, Hans, a passionate hunter, worked out of sheer necessity a possum line in an area known as the Jean D'Arcy Reserve. It was here that he first became aware that a large boar was afoot. Often hunting mates would stay with him, usually over a weekend; almost always they would get pigs. Before one of these trips Hans came across deep rooting, at least a metre deep. Like the deep tracks he had recently found, it indicated a big, mature animal. While this particular sign was still within the reserve, it was also very close to the Ahuahu Valley. The Ahuahu Stream, which drains into the Wanganui

River, has long been regarded as one of the top pig-hunting spots in the watershed.

At the end of May 1987, in the company of Simon Grey, and Jock and Nig Earston, Hans set off towards the Ahuahu Valley with the prime objective of finding the boar that had occupied his mind so much. They had seven dogs between them; Hans's trio were: Rip, a black and tan huntaway; Jake, a black cattle-dog; and big Dooley, a great Dane.

Well, it turned out that not only was the boar of a prodigious size but that he also had a top set of tusks to go with all of that muscle-packed bulk. Dooley found out about it — in a most painful fashion — when he made a real bad mistake and grabbed a solid hold of the black's one ear.

Whack!

Yelp!

'Shit!' That was Hans, of course.

When it was all over, Dooley was in a very bad way, glassy-eyed, whimpering, starting to wobble on his feet. Suddenly his legs buckled and down he went.

The boar was much too heavy to carry out — it was well in excess of 200 pounds — so they decided to take just the head and the back legs. Carrying Dooley, as Hans soon discovered, was no easy task: he weighed around 45 kilograms. After a short time, however, it was no longer necessary to carry him. Dooley had tangled with his last boar. One could not even hazard a guess at how many pig-dogs have died on the hill since the first wild boar and dog confronted each other in this country. Brave, perhaps foolhardy, dogs, giving their all, giving heaps. If only we gave as much in return.

Four weeks later Hans Brink was working on a fenceline near home. Because Rip and Jake were in sore need of a run, he had taken them with him, letting them range while he toiled. Now it was time for lunch and the dogs were missing. No matter, they wouldn't go far.

After lunch, Hans was walking past his woolshed when he heard barking coming from the direction of a nearby gully. Quickly, he released Buster (who belonged to Jock Earston), and, grabbing a knife, he then broke into a run.

In thick bush, Rip and Jake had bailed a black-and-white boar under a ponga. They were keeping a safe distance from him; the boar, glowering, was flashing his tusks. Hans paused, knife in hand. The boar weighed around 120 pounds and his tusks resembled pointed needles. He was, like most animals of that weight, young and very fast on his feet. In effect, he was like a lightweight boxer, quite capable of handing out a knockout blow.

With a name like Buster, Jock's dog could only be a holder. Holders are front-line warriors not known for discretion. They are bred to hold, to get stuck in, to mix it, to take a hammering, and to come up grinning. On seeing the black-and-white boar, Buster's brave heart had most likely leapt. Terrific! This was what living was all about.

While watching Rip and Jake intently, the black-and-white boar was also ready for Buster's charge. Wheeling, tusks flailing, the boar struck fast and hard. Buster reeled back, staggering, and then collapsed in an untidy heap. Hans had never seen a dog killed so swiftly before. Filled with burning rage, he snapped orders at his own dogs. It was a mistake. The boar, magnificent in close-quarters stuff, dispensed with Jake with a couple of perfectly timed blows and then turned his attention to Rip, who was soon spewing blood all over the place. With a triumphant snort, the boar escaped the battlefield.

Holding Jake's limp head in his hands, staring into his unseeing eyes, Hans Brink cursed his own stupidity. Two dogs killed today; Dooley a month ago. Why hadn't he brought his rifle? If he had, Jake would still be alive. He couldn't have saved Buster — he'd had no real control over Jock's dog. No matter what, Buster would have rushed in and maybe it would have been too tight in there to risk a shot. Maybe it would have all turned out the same. Hans took a deep breath and then released a long sigh.

Paid in Full

Stevensons Arm is a narrow peninsula on Lake Wanaka's eastern shoreline protecting a sheltered, channel-like inlet. The country directly east of this narrow stretch of water is dominated by Mount Burke's far-reaching shadow. It is appealing country, a mixture of golden tussocks, patchworks of scrub and topdressed pastureland. It is also likely pig country. However, until March 1988, and despite being widespread on both Mount Burke and Glen Dene stations, no pigs had been sighted there.

It is likely, then, that the boar that did find its way there had only recently done so. He had set up camp in an isolated belt of manuka that flourished in a grassy basin. The length of his residence could be perhaps estimated by the limited rooting he had carried out immediately around his lair and by the fact that none of it was very old, a week or, say, ten days at the very most. Precisely where he came from was naturally unclear, but we may presume that he had been born on either Mount Burke or Glen Dene stations. What was certain was that he was a mature pig, white in colour, weighing on the hoof around 300 pounds.

On a fine Sunday morning in late March the large boar was content in his self-imposed and not untypical isolation. After all, should the inclination to mate prove too strong to ignore, he knew where to find sows only too eager for a lengthy coupling.

On this same Sunday morning, Stuart Hewitt, who lived in the old stationhand's cottage on Mount Burke station and was on the property in that capacity, was mulling over where to go pig-hunting. Since arriving on the station with his wife, Shirley, in the previous December, he had hunted pigs a number of times with varying success.

As usual when such a hunt was on the cards, 55-year-old Stuart's mood was light and carefree. He had first hunted pigs as an 18-year-old in the Hokonui Hills, near his home town of Gore. Pigs were thick there, then. Later forays had taken him to the Blue Mountains, near Tapanui, and to western Southland, Blackmount station and Te Anau Downs. Great times! At no time since then had his love of the sport diminished. Pig-hunting was a part of his life, a vital part, and unless he hunted on a regular basis he became a little edgy, a shade depressed. He was like a man in need of a fix.

Shirley had recognised this trait in her husband early on; indeed, there was no way a perceptive person could have missed it. She had never tried to hold him back from his chosen sport, to curb his natural enthusiasm. All the same, there was a price to pay, and at times it seemed their lives revolved around Stuart's pig-hunting, his dogs, the next weekend's jaunt. With good-natured resignation, she often referred to herself as a pig widow. There have been a great many such pig widows in New Zealand.

Lingering over a second cup of tea, Stuart decided to have a look at a completely different part of the station from usual. It meant a short drive along the lakefront, more or less parallel to Stevensons Arm. The fact that no evidence of pigs had ever been seen there was of no real consequence. Sooner or later they would turn up.

Around mid-morning, he set off in his four-wheel-drive ute. He felt alive with anticipation as the land unfolded before him. It was a mood to match the weather, for the sun was spearing across the placid blue waters of the lake. He jolted harder than usual across a stockgrid and, fearing the worst, stole an apprehensive glance at his rifle. No worries. It was lodged securely across the passenger seat. A wry smile touched his weathered face as his pale blue eyes, like faded denim drying in the sun, settled momentarily on his P-14 .303. He and that rifle went back a very long way, to the 1950s, when wild pigs were never more numerous.

Of all the stations in the southern part of the South Island none was hit harder by the destructive antics of wild pigs than Blackmount station, at the south-east corner of the Takatimu Range, near Manapouri. In the 1950s pigs weren't on that run in their hundreds, they were in their many thousands. For a razor-keen young hunter like Stuart, and his equally enthusiastic mate, Brian Waddle, there was no finer place to spend a weekend than Blackmount station.

'Hey, those were the days, all right,' Stuart recalled wistfully one day. 'Me an' Brian used to leave home on a Friday evening and spend most of our weekends there — hell, you couldn't keep us away from the place. Pigs? Shit! They were everywhere. We'd get, oh, around sixty to eighty between us every time.

'One afternoon in the middle of the day I remember sitting down and overlooking a big gully. There must've been at least a hundred and fifty pigs in sight — everywhere you looked they'd be digging away in the fern. The place looked like it had been attacked from the air, you know.' He shook his head. 'Yeah, we saw the best of it, all right.'

At the time there was a national bounty scheme for wild pigs; in 1957, when Stuart was still hunting on Blackmount, the payment of bounties was as follows:

The Puketeraki Range, above the Waimakariri River.

MAF officer Russell Bryant looks out from the tail-end of the Criffel Range, across the valley of the upper Cardrona, to the Cardrona ski fields.

Graham Palamountain, aided by Chippy (foreground) and Sparky, checks out some fresh pig rooting.

The lovely Mangapurua Valley, deep in the Wanganui River backblocks.

Brendon Kelly, Mount Burke.

Stuart Hewitt, Mount Burke.

BSA Majestic .243, with tusks of the blackish-tan boar.

> A national bounty of one shilling or three rounds of .303 ammunition is paid for each wild pig killed, subject to the production of the animal's tail. The minimum number of tokens that may be accepted is ten and these must be fresh or dry and free from vermin. Hunters may submit tokens to any Forest Service office controlled by a Forest Ranger or more senior officer. Head office in Wellington will accept tokens.

Stuart continued, 'The Turnbull brothers owned Blackmount then, bloody good blokes they were, too. Never a problem getting on the place. Made sense, of course — you just couldn't ignore the pigs, else they'd take over the whole show. So everything was sweet as a bun until they sold out to a joker named, ah, yeah, Robertson, I think. Different story then — my word, yes! He reckoned he and his men could cope with the pigs.' He barked a brittle laugh, like old bones rubbing together. 'Fat chance of that happening!'

He paused, drumming fingers on a table, smiling reflectively at something he did not elaborate on. 'Anyway, I decided to hunt pigs full-time; you could get tenpence per pound for them. I knew there were still lots of pigs on Blackmount and so I put the hard word on them, said what I intended to do and could I come down there? They said, "Sure, anytime you like, the bastards are all over the show," and that's how I ended up on Blackmount again.'

Stuart was a married man by now; his daughter, Trish, was just two years old. Stuart would stay away from home working on Blackmount for up to six weeks at a time, have a couple of days home, then he'd be off again. He did that three winters in a row in the late 1950s and early 1960s. At tenpence per pound, providing he made the necessary effort, he could make good wages, better than working for a boss, anyway.

But pig-hunting full-time proved hard toil for both Stuart and his four-strong team of dogs. He had three experienced dogs and a likely up-and-coming youngster who, as he tagged along and observed, was expected to eventually graduate with honours. Stuart's main holder was Red, a top dog, a wee fella, great with kids and murder on pigs. Red was a mixture of boxer, bull-terrier and collie, the last breed dominating. There was also a collie cross called Tex.

A normal day's hunt would produce up to ten pigs, with the next day, and maybe a bit of the next too, taken up with carting out the carcasses. This was where a big, part draughthorse called Pinto came in. One time, Pinto was asked to perform the near impossible, to pack out in one load nine pigs, each weighing 40–80 pounds. The great-hearted packhorse didn't flinch as he set off with four pigs hanging from one side of the pack saddle and four from the other, with the remaining one lashed on top. Fortunately for Pinto it was all downslope.

During this three-year period it was perhaps surprising, under the circumstances, that Stuart lost only one dog to pigs. Even then the way it happened was extraordinary. They had come across a small mob of pigs in a high, rock-strewn gully. Tex, acting on his own (the other dogs had latched on to another pig), had grabbed a particularly pugnacious sow just behind her shoulder. She desperately tried to free herself from his tenacious grip. Squealing as though Stuart had jabbed a knife into her ribs, she started to run awkwardly, stumbling as the unaccustomed weight dragged down on her right side. Together they smashed through thick growth. The ground started to fall away sharply and, still locked together, they suddenly plunged jack-knifing into space, a sheer drop, Stuart recalls, of about five metres. They landed on piled-up boulders and both were killed instantly. Even today, so many years after it happened, Stuart's voice can soften when he recalls how Tex met his end.

Today, however, Stuart was on Mount Burke station and the name of the game was still wild pigs. But it was different from how it had been on Blackmount; he was without a regular team of pig-dogs. Not that he was without dogs — far from it. In the back of the ute, quite taken with the view and delighted to be out for a spin, were two black Labradors, one nine years old and the other a three-month-old pup, all wide-eyed and eager.

Stuart had had the older dog, Mike, since he was a pup. Mike was family, of course, your typically lovable Labrador, enjoying the water and wonderful with kids. Living on Mount Burke station was, where he was concerned, just the berries. The lake was only a mad scamper away and, close to the shore, he would swim back and forth for hours.

The opening day of the duck-hunting season was the highlight of his year and he was indispensable then. Chasing rabbits was good news, too. Now and then he'd retrieve from the Rakaia River a big Canada goose that his master, old sure-shot himself, had barrelled. That took some doing — leaping fearlessly into a rapid river and returning with a 10-pound bird in your mouth.

Near Stevensons Arm, Stuart clambered out of the ute. Mike whump-whumped his muscular tail on the ground, while Toby, after a swift pee, sniffed excitedly at fresh rabbit scratchings. With that old but ever-reliable P-14 tucked snugly in the crook of his arm, Stuart started up an easy slope. For a man in his mid-fifties, he was in fine shape, trimly built, at eleven stone, not a pound more, as he was fond of saying, than the day when he was married.

He increased his lengthy stride, feeling good, the stresses of working life starting to fall away, the years, too, so that, suddenly, he might again have been tightening the pack saddle on Pinto's back, calling out to his dogs, back on Blackmount station. He paused and scanned the undulating landscape methodically. He turned his gaze to Mount Gold's impressive 1286-metre peak. It was tough country, chamois range (he'd taken a top buck up there). You certainly wouldn't expect to see pigs up there among the bluffs, scampering around like well-seasoned mountaineers wearing crampons. Incredible! They had been feeding on snowgrass, he had discovered, big clumps uprooted, that or speargrass. There wasn't much else on the menu up there.

Stuart stopped reflecting on pigs that reckoned they were Austrian chamois and, with a lift of the shoulders, started to sidle a gentle hillface. Soon it petered out and he was looking into a sheltered basin, a patch of manuka the size of your average suburban section. His breath quickening, he spotted the black scars of rooting almost at once. He almost ran downslope. The rooting was nearly a metre deep, indicating a large pig. It was freshly done, too — he figured it could be from the night before.

Both dogs were eagerly checking out the rooting. Lifting his head, Mike looked curiously at his master. Mike had been kept well away from pigs until now; he wouldn't know what a boar was if one butted his backside.

Stuart turned his attention to the heavy scrub, then turned to Mike. Why not?

'Get in there!'

Mike had heard that command many times and he sprang forward as though he was going after a mallard. Young Toby went to follow his hero, but Stuart grabbed him by the collar. Of course, Mike soon came across a very big black-and-white boar dozing in his comfortable bed. He barked loudly — gee, wasn't this fun! The boar lumbered to his feet and snorted as if something were blocking his nose.

Stuart waited, suddenly edgy and tense. A frantic commotion came from within the cover; still Mike barked, the tone changing. Stuart cursed: he couldn't see a darn thing. The boar's snorting became a horrendous sound, Mike yelped, and Stuart groaned as though in pain.

At a dead run, tail lodged between his legs, Mike exited the scrub. There was no sound, a hushed silence at once ominous. Backing away, rifle at the ready, Stuart went to Mike's side. There was a wound in Mike's neck that didn't look too serious. Stuart was filled with self-recrimination: it was a fool's trick to put Mike onto a boar! The wound would require cleaning and a few stitches. A quick but thorough examination of the rest of Mike's body revealed no further damage. It could, Stuart knew, have ended entirely differently.

Still there was no sound from the boar. Only a good team of pig-dogs would shift him, Stuart knew. He suddenly thought about Red and Tex, long gone now. Red ended his days in easy retirement on a farm down south and Tex . . . poor old Tex. He looked grimly at the boar's patch of scrub. It was too thick by half; there was no way he was about to go in there. He'd already made one bad mistake today, and there was no point in compounding it. Trailed by his dogs, Stuart climbed out of the sheltered hollow.

What had happened to Mike played on Stuart's mind over the next week, although Mike had recovered quickly. The next weekend arrived, and with it his first opportunity to return to the basin. The trouble was that Sunday was cold and bleak, with low clouds and a nasty wind whipping across the lake. Stuart somehow curbed his impatience. It would have to be next week.

Much to Stuart's relief, the following weekend was warm and sunny; the tall tussocks were motionless and a few puffy white clouds, like becalmed sailboats, barely moved in a sky of deepest blue. Stuart wasn't too confident the boar would still be there as, with eager steps, he neared the well-hidden basin. Now, late in the morning, it was a suntrap. But, yes, that was fresh rooting over there, which meant the boar was almost certainly there right now.

He weighed his options. From his grassy knoll he had a clear view of the entire basin and there was no way the boar could leave the scrub without being seen. Somehow he had to spook it out. Reaching out a hand, he dislodged a partly concealed rock the size of a golfball. He lobbed it into the scrub.

Silence.

He found another rock close to hand, bigger, a dummy hand grenade. That too was suddenly airborne. This time there was an immediate reaction. The manuka shook wildly, then, right in front of where Stuart was kneeling, the boar broke cover. It stood there, glowering, with its huge head down.

The sheer size of the boar took Stuart's breath away; it was by far the largest he had ever seen. To think he had encouraged Mike to tackle that! For once his P-14 seemed a mistake, the hollow-point bullet totally inadequate.

Suddenly the boar was aware of danger. Stuart aimed, lodging the front sight in the rear sight, the muzzle pointing downslope, directly at the boar's head. The animal, its life in a delicate balance, started to wheel about.

Thu-unck! The booming roar of the .303 reverberated around the small sunny basin. Gradually the sound faded away, the last, lingering echo high up. Shakily, Stuart stood up and went to the boar's side, ready to shoot if necessary, but the boar was still, eyes unfocused. Stuart thought about Mike. Paid in full, he thought with satisfaction.

Where a Big Boar Lurks

It was a very warm day in early winter 1991. At the stationhand's cottage on Mount Burke station, Shirley Hewitt was placing a heavily laden tray on a wooden table positioned on a narrow veranda. To the east there was a fine view of the spine-like backbone of the property and, as I sat there, enjoying the warmth of the sun, two paradise ducks flew overhead.

'. . . so, yeah, that's pretty much the story of how I got the big fella,' Stuart said with a faraway look, in the way that bushmen the world over are apt to do.

'Milk?'

'Huh?' I too must have been lost in thought.

Stuart gestured expansively towards the mountains. 'Great spot, isn't it?' It wasn't really a question. He shook his head and added, 'Never get tired of it, y'know.'

I knew what he meant; the mountains, like the sea, are forever changing. Today the high, craggy peaks he had indicated were sun-hazed, almost unreal, like a half-recalled dream.

'Yeah . . .' Stuart continued after a lengthy pause. 'A man could live here forever, I guess.' He sighed heavily.

I quietly sipped my coffee and ate some fruitcake. Then, catching Stuart's attention, I asked if the black-and-white boar was the biggest he had taken on the station.

He nodded, then turned his face again to the mountains. Again he motioned grandly, a sweep of a hand that included Mount Gold, Mount Maude and Quartz Creek. 'You know, there might be an even bigger boar over there.'

Now, I couldn't leave that there, could I?

As with the huge black-and-white boar, there was no way of knowing how long the boar had been inhabiting the low, frontal country below Mount Gold and Mount Maude. Quartz Creek lay beyond Alan and Jan

Gillespie's 345-hectare farm, bypassing it before meandering across Mount Burke station to merge with Stevensons Arm. In and around the creek were pleasant, sun-warmed hillfaces, scrubby little gullies that retained the heat of a summer's day long after the sun had retreated behind the ranges, and large but isolated patches of fern and bracken. Given the choice, few pigs would turn up their dirt-crusted snouts at residing there.

Forest Service and, later, DoC wild pig control operations had proved profitable in the area. Some good-sized boars had been taken there, but no truly large boar had, by the mid 1980s, been sighted. It is difficult to say precisely who was the first to sight it. Perhaps it was John Fleming or Paul Hondelink on one of their infrequent forays; possibly it was another of the government strike force on pig control work. Maybe it was Stuart Hewitt himself — he often hunted or worked there, frequently with Brendon Kelly. You couldn't overlook Don Ramsey, a musterer on the place about the time Brendon Kelly had first turned up there in 1985. Apparently Ramsey had come across the tracks of a huge boar mixed in with the hoofmarks of a number of smaller animals. Collectively, they had completely uprooted a ferny hillface.

But most likely it was Johnny Hollows, a butcher from Wanaka. One day in Quartz Creek Hollows was close to two boars: one mature, one not. It was the younger and much smaller one that revealed itself first and paid the penalty. Hollows, working the bolt of his rifle frantically, saw a far bigger animal break from cover moments later. It powered downslope fast, like a bobsled gaining speed with every corner. Nevertheless, he'd had sufficient time to see its distinctive blackish-tan colour. While his dogs gave frantic chase, they had been unable to check the boar's pell-mell escape.

That the blackish-tan boar was in the company of a much younger animal was not surprising. Of course, the younger fellow might have been there for nothing more than companionship; the real reason, however, was more likely twofold. Boars only reach full maturity — around five years — if they are basic survivors. As they mature they learn that their life is fraught with danger; in some parts it may be from wolves, saltwater crocodiles or tigers, but mostly it is from the ultimate predator, man.

To avoid danger a boar will apply all sorts of cunning ruses; he might, for instance, range the dense European woods with a much younger companion. When ringed by beaters, the older boar is somehow able to persuade the younger one to reveal itself. In the resulting mêlée, the old boar is very often able to break through the line of baffled beaters and riflemen to escape; his decoy having paid the price for his incaution or gullibility.

It is worth noting that very much the same thing happens with members of the deer family; sika and fallow deer are two prime examples. Often during the vulnerable mating season they will have a younger stag with them. Many a too-eager deerhunter has put down an insignificant beast in thick cover only to see, several agonising seconds later, a trophy-bearing animal bounding scornfully away.

On Mount Burke station, then, and in the general district for that matter, word started to spread that there was an unusually large boar ranging the run's south-eastern corner. Talk of the boar naturally lured Stuart Hewitt to Quartz Creek. There, well beyond range of his open-sighted .303, he saw three boars and what he judged was a single sow. They were rooting up the ground with untold enthusiasm. One of the boars appeared much bigger than its companions and matched almost perfectly the general description that Johnny Hollows had given of the boar.

He was built on powerful lines. Weighed on the hoof, he might have tipped the scales close to, or possibly beyond, the 300-pound mark, depending on the season and how well he had been eating. He carried a magnificent set of tusks; they were almost unmarked, wickedly sharp fighting implements, thick at the base and honed to perfection. They protruded about $3^1/_2$ inches.

The boar became something of an obsession for Stuart Hewitt. Often in the company of Brendon Kelly, sometimes alone, he went searching for it. Once, with Brendon Kelly, he got very close to it, but the boar broke just before they reached the tangled spot where their dogs had bailed it up. The boar — in typical fashion — ran in the direction that gave him the advantage, downslope.

Jan Gillespie's meeting with the huge blackish-tan boar was unique. In the autumn of 1986, Jan, then in her early thirties, decided to go for one of her regular runs while Alan worked on a fenceline near their northern boundary with Mount Burke station. She was feeling good and the very last thing on her mind as she cut around a sharp bend on the track was a pig. Certainly not a massive boar, anyway! They were so close together on the track that eye contact was made.

'Eck!' Jan cried.

The boar, finding the experience equally shocking, rumbled deep in his belly and, turning, bolted off the track. Terrified, Jan ran on. The trouble was, the boar was now running a little ahead of her on a parallel course, its great head twisted slightly so that it was watching her out of the corner of its eye.

Jan's mind raced with endless possibilities. What if the boar suddenly altered course and charged her? What was her chance of escaping injury? In one sickening word — none! Heart hammering and throat dry, Jan whirled off the track and darted like a hare through the low, scrubby growth. She half expected the boar to give chase, but there was no sound of pursuit.

She was still shaken when she spotted the boundary fence. As she angled towards it, knowing that Alan wasn't too far away, two adult red deer suddenly appeared right in front of her and, with loud 'woofing!' sounds, rocketed off. It was definitely not her day, Jan thought, as she recovered from the latest shock. Clambering over the fence, it occurred to her that Alan wasn't going to believe any of this!

One blustery winter's day in 1987, Brendon Kelly and his 13-year-old son, Nathan, went hunting high on Mount Gold's brawny, tussock-clad shoulder. Brendon, in his mid thirties, had grown up around Palmerston, Otago. He had been a dedicated pig-hunter for years, as are many of Otago's brave sons. Popular haunts of his had included the famed Silver Peaks, Shag Valley station and the country around Dunback, all fine pig-hunting territory before red deer were introduced in the early 1870s. With his strong, 85-kilogram frame, uncompromising blue eyes, short-cropped hair and bushy beard, Brendon Kelly personified the rugged individualistic nature of the early Irish settlers that, given time, became musterers and pig-hunters.

Father and son, in companionable silence, were still high on the upper slopes of Mount Gold when Sam, a bull-terrier cross, suddenly paused. He sniffed the ground and, wagging his tail, became excited. It was with good reason, for the tracks were almost certainly those of 'the boar'. Moreover, they were fresh enough to indicate that the boar might have winded or sensed them and, taking evasive action, had moved into thickish cover.

With a sudden, sideways leap, Sam was off the track and following the boar's tracks into a riot of interlocked growth. Good dog, Sam — game as they come. Out of sight, yet still close, Sam barked sharply; again he barked, this time a short way further on, lower down. Then silence. Still, it was encouragement enough to send big Hoss, a bull-mastiff, barrelling after him. But Hoss checked himself before reaching the fringe of the cover and then, very much out of character, trotted back to rejoin his master.

With a wondering expression, Brendon Kelly stared long and hard at his dog.

'What's up with him, Dad?' an equally puzzled Nathan questioned.

Brendon shrugged. 'Buggered if I know, Son.' He smiled without humour. 'Maybe he knows something we don't, eh?'

Maybe big Hoss did at that.

Father and son, growing increasingly concerned, listened in vain to hear Sam reveal his whereabouts. There was still no sign of him as the evening closed in and, fearing the worst, they returned home.

Every evening after work for a full week, Brendon Kelly returned to the area they had last seen Sam and Kelly fired shot after shot. He left a heap of his unwashed clothing on a track, hoping that Sam might come across it and, recognising the smell, wait there to be picked up. But Sam had vanished off the face of the earth.

There is no doubt in Brendon Kelly's mind that Sam had tangled with the blackish-tan boar and had been killed. He still remembers Sam the bull-terrier cross. With affection, too.

Only with a Spotlight

During 1988, John Fleming's work on pig control took him back to Quartz Creek; here, at last, he saw pig sign consistent with that of the boar he had heard so much about. By this time Mac, his faithful curly-coated retriever, was giving thirteen a hard nudge in the shoulder. Worse, Mac was deaf, the result of having countless shots fired close to his head. It was an unfair price to pay for years of unflinching service.

On pigs, Mac still rated; he could still find and bail just about any pig. Often, John was able to work him with hand actions or signals. The problem was that Mac had to be looking in Fleming's direction to see them, which in most instances was in the opposite direction to where the game — deer, goat or pig — actually was. On the subject of goats, Mac could not be controlled anymore. Feral goats were rated top priority by DoC, and a dog that could not perform — under complete control — was a direct liability.

Recently, John Fleming had started to think about giving Mac away. Not an easy decision to reach, but perhaps a sensible one. He knew a young chap who was keen to start a pig-dog pack. Greg Ronald, a musterer on Waiponi station, near Dunedin, would give Mac a good home. Moreover, there would be no need for Mac to stop hunting. From what young Ronald said, there were heaps of pigs on Waiponi. Yes, better that than the alternative, being cooped up in a kennel every day in Hawea. That was the last thing Mac deserved.

In the course of his work around Quartz Creek, John Fleming saw the same large, deeply imprinted tracks of the boar over a wide area. The boar seemed to be almost always on the move, constantly shifting camp, never lingering long, the mark of one who survives. Towards the end of his allotted time there, during which Mac had worked exceptionally well on pigs and Meg, Mac's six-month-old pup, had taken it all in like a child that has suddenly learned to read, Fleming came across the now-familiar spoor of an extra-large boar. *The* boar, he knew. Better still, the sign was fresh enough to cause his pulse to quicken. He rose from the distinct hoof-marks and cast a searching eye around him. The terrain wasn't too steep and most of it was under heavy cover. A fine spot for a boar to rest up during the heat of the day.

Meantime, Mac was working hard. Sniffing the ground, testing the air . . . getting the general feel of things. Meg watched her father with fascination. She seemed so proud of him. Mac worked over the ground while Fleming waited, his .222 rifle in the crook of his arm.

Mac tensed; his body quivered. A pig was near! Mac sprang into a hard, driving run, doing what he still did best. Meg hung back; Fleming wasn't in the least bit surprised. Not too long ago she had been given a sobering lesson.

A few weeks ago Mac had bailed a black boar — a good 200-pounder — and Meg, wildly excited, had joined in the ruckus. Soon both Mac and his daughter had got out of sight. There had been a deep grunt from the boar, followed by an equally loud whooshing sound and a high-pitched yelp from young Meg. Meg had exited that patch of thick growth as though fired from a cannon, her tail tucked firmly between her legs. Cowering, but unhurt, she had stood close enough to John Fleming's legs to touch him. The boar had broken then; Mac gave chase, barking once. Three times Mac had stopped that particular animal. It did not break a fourth time.

Now, in Quartz Creek, Mac had vanished into thick growth. He barked insistently and John Fleming had a strong hunch he had found the boar asleep. By the sound of things the boar was very wide awake now. Fleming barrelled into the tangled growth. To his amazement, Meg rushed past him. She obviously had a short memory. He could only hope she did not get hurt.

Again Mac barked. A pig snorted.

Fleming felt something brushing against his leg — Meg, with her tail between her legs and apprehension stamped on her face. Obviously she wanted nothing at all to do with the boar after seeing it at close range. She was learning fast.

As John Fleming moved closer to the unseen boar, now, he judged, only metres away, adrenalin surged through his body. Again Mac demanded immediate action.

The boar made a strange sort of growling sound deep in its throat; it was loaded with genuine menace. As never before, John Fleming was fearful for the safety of his dog. Rifle cocked, held at the port arms position, he warily parted some low branches, and immediately caught sight of a big, blocky shape. Perhaps aware of a new twist in the proceedings, the blackish-tan boar powered off with the whooshing sound, a great expulsion of pent-up breath, that John had heard other boars make in the same situation.

Mac brought the boar to a halt several more times before he realised the inevitable: that it would break on him every single time.

By the winter of 1989 the same boar, a supreme opportunist, was occasionally visiting the Gillespies' small farm to partake of one of his favourite meals: the carcass of a lamb. The carcasses could often be seen in the low-lying paddocks, pitifully limp bundles seeming to shrink before one's eyes. They would be watched over by their mothers until it became clear a miracle wasn't going to happen.

To reach the Gillespie place the boar had to cross the boundary of Mount Burke station, marked by rabbit-proof fencing that had stood there, dug into the ground, since the mid 1950s. While it presented a formidable barrier to rabbits, to the boar it posed no obstacle at all. He simply put his head down and smashed his way through. Alan Gillespie, with his sheep escaping through the newly made gaps and mixing with Cotty Burdon's animals, was not impressed.

During this particular winter, Stuart Hewitt spent a great deal of time searching for the boar. He soon came to realise that the boar was ranging a wide area and that it never approached Gillespie's farm from the same direction. It didn't use the holes in the fence that Alan had been unable to attend to; it did not smash through holes Alan had fixed. It simply created new ones, sometimes, as it wandered back and forth between the two properties, making as many as ten holes in a night.

To digress a little: research into the patterns of behaviour of the European wild boar has revealed that it is deeply mistrustful of man. The adult wild boar will live mostly alone out of the mating season, although he may allow a younger boar to travel with him. He moves about more in the late evening, overnight, and in the early morning; he rests under cover during the more vulnerable hours. Should he be in heavily hunted country, which means most of Europe, he will frequently alter his itinerary — only rarely will he adhere to fixed trails or paths. Our blackish-tan boar, while he lived in an entirely different habitat to the European wild boar and was probably descended from Asian wild stock, was merely displaying the characteristic traits of *Sus scrofa*.

Stuart Hewitt had no luck that winter, and in the winter of 1990 the boar still foraged on dead lambs and the remains of sickly sheep on Gillespie's farm. Instead of removing all the carcasses, Alan Gillespie made a point of leaving some of them there, to lure the boar to a set place. At night he and Brendon Kelly, who lived nearby, hunted the boar with the aid of a spotlight, but they had no success.

In the summer the blackish-tan boar ranged the high country behind Gillespie's farm, often venturing into Mount Burke's back paddocks. No one could catch him; the boar seemed invincible.

It was June 1991, and with my mind full of huge wild boars, I gunned the car along the unsealed road that linked the Hewitts' place with State

Highway 6. I had passed the cottage where Brendon and Karen Kelly lived. Now I was driving past the Mount Burke boundary fence. On Alan and Jan Gillespie's green acres sheep were grazing, they were at peace, most heavy with lamb.

On a whim, I stopped. I got out and looked beyond the sheep . . . up to the territory of the huge boar. It was early afternoon and it was lovely and warm; I reckoned he would be resting somewhere up there where the rolling hills began. Maybe luck would run out for the boar this coming winter.

Perhaps a week later the long run of mild, unseasonal weather came to a sudden end, replaced by the beginning of a very severe winter. In Alexandra the temperature would drop below zero for days on end as the sun tried in vain to break through the heavy cloud. The locals had to contend with a seemingly unending hoar frost. Motorists from one end of Otago to the other faced perhaps the worst black ice ever seen in the region. The panelbeaters profited and the insurance companies didn't.

So cold were overnight temperatures that sheep froze by their wool to the ground and were trapped until assistance came, if it came. Near Queenstown the Shotover River froze solid from bank to bank; it had not done so in over a hundred years. Deep snow blocked major highways from Milford to Arthur's Pass. Throughout the region stock — sheep, cattle, deer — relied on handouts of, mostly, hay. Meantime, in Twizel the highest temperature in three weeks was 1°C; there were twenty hoar frosts in twenty-one days.

Also in the Mackenzie Country, rabbits were having a ghastly time of it. There was nothing to eat after the pine plantations in the region had been virtually destroyed. Rabbits without ears became a common sight, but, contrary to popular claims, it was not cannibalism but frostbite that was the cause. John Robertson, a MAF technology scientist, estimated that up to 50 percent of the rabbit population in the eastern Mackenzie Basin perished from intense cold and lack of food, and that those that had survived had lost as much as 45 percent of their body weight.

The runholders who in the past had run more rabbits than sheep were naturally ecstatic over this; after all, the local Pest Destruction boys had never achieved such a kill rate. Unfortunately the rabbit, like the wild pig, is a born survivor. The rabbits that saw out the winter of 1991 were the super-strong, the finest specimens, incredibly resilient. They would form the nucleus of the future generations of rabbits that, given time, would undoubtedly spring up again in the eastern Mackenzie Basin.

What then, runholder?

At nearly 9 p.m. on a June weeknight, Brendon Kelly was in no mood for television. Rising from his chair, he went outside. A mixture of snow and ice-laced rain was falling. He had searched without success for the blackish-tan boar last night, for it was known to be feeding on a carcass

Alan Gillespie had deliberately left alone. Oblivious to the biting cold, watching the snow falling in the light spilling out through the open doorway, he suddenly had a powerful premonition that his luck would change tonight. Kelly went inside and picked up the telephone. He rang Alan Gillespie. Was he up to a bit of spotlighting? After three years of fixing holes in the fencing Alan was always ready for a hunting trip.

The ute growled in low gear across the icy paddocks. Alan Gillespie, driving, allowed his eyes to follow the brighter-than-day beam of the 12-volt spotlight that Brendon Kelly, standing on the back, held in gloved hands. The icy wind whipped at Kelly's face, stinging his eyes. He steeled himself against the cold and watched where he played the light.

They crossed a hollow and swept past an offal pit the boar knew all about. The boar knew about the carcass of a ewe near this spot, too. In all probability he was gorging himself there when, suddenly, he sensed that danger was about.

Working the spotlight back and forth, Brendon Kelly, numb with cold, saw it illuminate the carcass. His heart leapt: it had definitely been worried. The spotlight flashed over a patch of scrub, the only cover in a large area, just the place for . . . something moved in there. Alan saw it, too. Something big — wrong — something very, very big.

The blackish-tan boar lunged into a run. Anticipating its direction, Gillespie, working the gearstick smoothly and quickly, headed off the boar so that it swung back towards open ground. Spinning the steering wheel, he went after the boar. For a moment he caught the boar in his headlight.

What a size! Brendon Kelly tried to aim his .243 at the fleeing, bobbing target. Going full tilt, the boar started to pull away from the roaring monster, seemingly right behind it. About forty paces separated machine and beast when Kelly fired — cra-a-ck! — and the boar, hit between its shoulder blades, faltered and then nosedived to the earth.

Elated, Gillespie braked so hard that Kelly was very nearly thrown off the back. Regaining his balance, and some of his composure, Kelly leapt to the ground, his rifle already reloaded. He aimed and shot the boar again, a sound precaution. But there was no response whatsoever when the 100-grain projectile smashed into the boar's limp body.

The men gazed in awe at the boar. Later, they would measure it and discover it was six feet from nose to tail and that, dressed-out, it weighed 235 pounds. Previously, Brendon Kelly had never taken a boar that weighed, dressed-out or not, in excess of 200 pounds.

For the record, John Fleming gave old Mac to musterer Greg Ronald. He heard later that Ronald had moved elsewhere — a station near Clinton, perhaps. Mac? He has no idea what happened to him. A dog's life, right?

The Mighty Quinn

Whatever their size — Grant Batty or Colin Meads — rugby legends stand tall in the company of ordinary men. This is equally true of other sports; in sheep shearing, for instance, no one has ever stood taller than Alexandra-based Brian 'Snow' Quinn.

Today, Snow Quinn is fifty years old and deep lines have added character to a strong, weathered face. The blue eyes are direct and the rangy body, nudging 1.90 metres (unusually tall for a shearer), still whipcord lean. Physically, he appears little different from those heady days when, between 1965 and 1972, he won the Golden Shears championship a record-breaking six times. It is considered unlikely that such a marvellous achievement will ever be surpassed.

Much, of course, has already been written about this and the many other records the tall man set. Oddly enough, nothing has ever been written about the other passion in his life. It gripped him as a teenager in New Plymouth, and more than thirty-five years down the track pig-hunting is still a compelling part of Snow Quinn's life.

A light mist, thicker about the rolling, rabbit-denuded tops, covered Central Otago. A few specks of rain were falling, more of a promise than the real thing. It was cold enough to wear thermal underwear and a heavy woollen shirt.

At the bottom of a long gully on Timburn station, near Tarras, wild pigs, in quest of grubs, worms, roots, whatever, had upturned the black earth near a fenceline. Turning away from the rooting, Snow Quinn, with a rising look of anticipation about him, rasped the back of a hand across his stubbly jaw and pointed out it was only a few hours old. His younger brother Colin, also a shearer, did not disagree. The sign, resembling a mortar attack on a carpet of vivid greenery, was consistent with a mob of pigs recently seen near here, higher in the gully, by a full-time rabbiter employed on the station.

Timburn, founded in around 1916, carries 11,000 merino sheep, 450 high-ranging Hereford cattle, small numbers of predominantly ginger pigs, a fair number of California quail, and, out on Mount Misery, enough rabbits to make it necessary for a shepherd to belt them out of the way with his hillstick.

John 'Tussock' Lucas, the runholder, was in Alexandra a few days later and happened to meet up with Snow Quinn, who, after living there for twenty-eight years, is the town's favourite adopted son. Snow's association with Timburn went back ten years or so, to about the time pigs had really settled into that part of the country. Naturally enough the conversation had turned to pigs. John mentioned that the boys were going out Sunday morning after the pigs the rabbiter had seen and also a larger mob observed recently by Willie 'Wong' Cowie, a local fencing contractor and diehard pig-hunter.

'Maybe you should go along,' John suggested.

'They won't mind?'

'No worries, Snow.'

The boys in question were: John's sons, thirteen-year-old Ben and seventeen-year-old Sam; Hamish Cameron, a seventeen-year-old shepherd on the place; and eighteen-year-old James Lucas, son of Gordon Lucas (a cousin of John's), who owned nearby Nine Mile station. So there we all were on Sunday morning, early. Seven men and heaps of dogfaces. Not quite a three-ring-circus, but getting uncomfortably close to it.

Despite his forays on the station, Snow had never hunted this particular gully. From below it appeared extremely tight, a gash weaving between bare hills. The steep rocky sides and bottom were choked with sweet briar and tangled with matagouri. It was, above all else, the sweet briar that lured pigs here in the autumn and early winter. On this particular day the low-growing bushes were heavy with fruit.

The dogs exploded from their cages on the back of Snow's 1966 Land-Rover. Among the dogs was Sam, a ten-year-old collie cross that Snow had raised from a pup. Sam's fifteen-month-old son, Pal, was out of a huntaway bitch, as were the two up-and-coming youngsters that completed the team. Still Snow appeared unsure.

'What's it like higher up?' he asked Sam Lucas.

'Much more open,' was the reply.

Snow swallowed that slowly, as if he was unsure of the taste, and then said, 'Much rather hunt downhill at my age than the other way around.' His slight smile was rueful.

'Know what you mean,' I said with feeling.

'Piece of piss!' was Colin's contribution.

'We can drive to the top?' Snow again looked at young Sam.

'No problem.' Sam indicated a handy ridge.

While it did make sense to work down the gully I had a powerful hunch the pigs would still be close and I put words to those thoughts.

'That's what I reckon, too,' Colin said.

The young guys shuffled their feet and said nothing.

Snow showed his teeth in a tight, mirthless grimace.

'Let's go find out then, eh?'

With that he started off with long, easy strides, a .303 rifle slung across his shoulder.

There were fresh slots etched on a sheep trail and pig sign — young stuff, Snow reckoned. The dogs fanned out ahead, sniffing the ground, taking a hurried pee but not, sensibly, by cocking a leg on a sharp-barbed matagouri bush. Up a low ridge we went; it overlooked the gully.

I have participated in a number of pig-hunts. Most have been successful, that is to say we have taken game. But even when pigs weren't forthcoming, I have always learned something from my considerably more experienced companions, men and dogs alike. At no time, however, has the action started faster than it did that late May morning. Perhaps three minutes after leaving the vehicles, the dogs were off like shots from a twelve-bore shotgun. At once the men gave chase, uphill at a fast run.

In his book *The Game Animals of New Zealand* T. E. Donne has this to say in a lengthy segment on wild pigs:

> There is perhaps no tougher work anywhere than hunting wild boar on the mountains of New Zealand. They resort to the most difficult, deep, rugged, rough gullies which are thickly covered with brush and undergrowth interlaced with strong lawyer vines which tear the hunter's face, hands, and clothing.
>
> Pig hunting is for the young, agile athlete, for when grey hairs tinge the temples the sport is too strenuous for lungs and legs.

Heart pounding, I weaved between clumps of sweet briar and patches of matagouri that plucked at my clothing. Then, to my relief, the ground shelved off. I paused, breathing heavily, running splayed fingers through my greying hair. And there ——

A boar was dropping off the main ridge in a secretive fashion. In no real hurry, swat-like tail swinging in time with its gait, the brownish-coated animal vanished over a grassy spur and started, I suspected, down to the creek. Moments later Sam appeared and he too crossed the grassy spur. Meantime, Pal and Colin's two dogs were in hot pursuit of another pig; the young guys were hollering like a Sioux raiding party as they and Colin brought up the rear.

With Sam closing in fast, the boar suddenly checked itself this side of the creek and backed hard, a rear-end shuffle, against a patch of scrub. Like blowflies attracted to carrion, Snow's other dogs arrived to join in the ruckus.

Like nimble-footed Snow, I scrambled the sharp, slippery descent to the

Snow Quinn and Sam look across to Cluden station.

From left: Shearing legend Brian 'Snow' Quinn; Colin Quinn's blue heeler; and Colin Quinn, Snow's brother.

Pigs range high on Timburn station and often it's simply a case of glassing for them.

Some things never change when you're chasing pigs — carrying them out of steep gullies, as James Lucas is doing, is one of them.

Hamish Cameron pauses in the 'fat lamb' paddock. Only rabbits put on weight here.

On the lower slopes of the Pisa Range, Colin Ashmore looks across the Clutha Valley to the snow-clad Dunstan Mountains.

While Gary Walker chats with an unseen Colin Ashmore, Ros Moseby attends to an unconscious Butch's wounds.

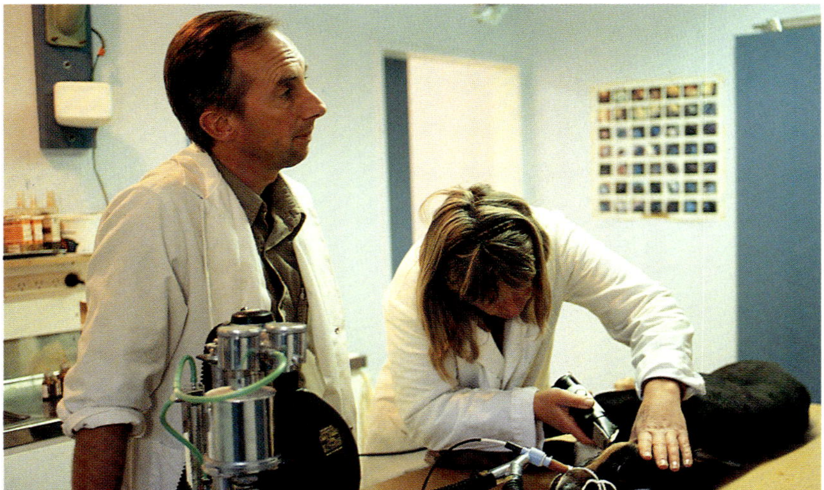

creek. The boar was putting on a brave face and making enough racket for a styful of porkers. He wasn't about to win this battle: he had a major handicap, a lack of adequate weapons. One tusk, perhaps as a result of fighting, had been snapped off at the base and the other one was stumpy — more rounded than pointed. He was no danger, and the dogs knew it.

Knife in hand, Snow edged alongside the boar's rear. His dogs, revelling in it, grabbed at already torn ears, at folds of wrinkled, loose skin hanging under the thick neck. A clinically delivered thrust of the blade brought the one-sided contest to a swift result.

Snow had gutted the boar — about 90 pounds — when a grinning James arrived.

'Got a small ginger pig,' James explained.

Snow suggested that James carry the carcass out to the vehicle; brawny James shrugged and with a grunt hoisted the kill onto his back.

On the ridgetop, sweating freely, James linked up with Sam, who was loaded down with the other carcass, and with young Ben tagging along they set off down the ridge.

'Good young jokers,' Snow reckoned with a grin and a nod at their retreating backs.

Meanwhile, Pal, a devil for work, had taken off up the gully and Colin and his two dogs, both blue heeler crosses, went after him; the eventual result was one more small ginger pig. Snow, Hamish and I crossed a gently sloping hillface to meet the young guys, driving the vehicles, at a prearranged spot.

A few chinks of blue were starting to break up the otherwise slate grey sky when, in Indian file, we traversed a particularly hard-hit stretch of country. Mostly it was bare rock and grey flaky earth that gave the impression it would kill for a decent rainfall. All that did well on this slope were sweet briar and, surprisingly, plump rabbits.

'Amazing,' I said, tapping Snow on the shoulder.

'This is the fat lamb paddock,' was Snow's droll comment.

Later we met up with Colin and a cheerful-looking Pal.

'How'd you make out?' Snow asked.

'Got one.'

'And . . .'

'By the time I got there it wasn't worth packing out.'

Snow shrugged; there was nothing you could do about that.

Following our early success, it was late afternoon before we caught up with the pigs the fencing contractor had brought to John's attention. By then the sun was out of hiding and the magnificent country was glowing in a burnished light. The pigs had set up camp on high ground, facing the rising sun. It had, over the years, been extensively topdressed and it had done wonders for the rampant thistles.

From a vantage point on an outcrop of rock, I had a bird's eye view of events. I saw the dogs converge on a patch of manuka scrub and almost immediately a dark-coated sow with survival on her terrified mind burst into the open and, without breaking stride, charged downhill. From within the scrub a horrendous scream rang out: another junior-sized pig had just run out of luck. A small ginger pig broke out of the heavy growth and, instead of following in mother's tracks, it started to angle around the hillface. A second little reddish pig appeared and went after its brother or sister. Two little porkers off to the country fair.

Then Sam was in the open, and I knew that one, if not two, more little pigs were going to die. Quickly, Sam located their scent. The last little pig was topping a ridge perhaps 80 metres away; it dropped out of sight. Moments later Sam topped the same spot.

'Sam, get out of there!' That was Snow, nearby.

Sam hesitated.

'Sam — you bastard! Get back here!'

Sam came bounding uphill like a pig-dog half his age.

'No point in taking all the young ones, is there?' explained Snow soon after.

'Agreed,' I said. 'Besides, small pigs turn into big pigs.'

'Exactly.' The tall man known as the Mighty Quinn laughed.

Later, as evening fell on a successful pig-hunt on Timburn station, I gazed at a stunning panorama of bare brown hills to the north and west. Turning to Snow Quinn, I asked him what station that was.

'Cluden. Neil Purvis owns it. Top place.' Snow added that it covered 15,700 hectares and was a place he had often hunted with success.

The sun was low now, casting a golden, honey-like hue on those rabbit-infested slopes known as the Dunstan Mountains. It hardly looked like pig habitat, but there are few environments where the animal can't make a go of it. Looking more carefully, it was possible to see that it wasn't total desolation fit only for rabbits. There were patches of tussock scattered about and clumps of manuka and sweet briar made out in shallow little gullies. Pigs could scratch out a living of sorts, mostly foraging on the red berries of sweet briar and, at a pinch, they could always dig up rabbit burrows. Indeed, some pigs are such expert rabbiters that I'm rather surprised the Pest Destruction Board doesn't put them on the payroll.

Taken all round, Snow Quinn has had an enviable run with his pig-dogs.

'I've found if you can keep 'em till they're three years old,' he says, 'you don't seem to have too much trouble after that.'

Later, Snow would tell me about some of the experiences he shared with his dogs.

Kim was perhaps his first pig-dog of note. She was a boxer cross, brindled white in colour, and came to the south via a shearing mate in Rotorua. Of medium size, she was both a finder and a holder, as game as they come, and intelligent enough not to hold until her master arrived on the action-packed scene. Kim did not say no to a good-looking collie and one of the resulting puppies was a most appealing youngster with a big black patch on his lower back and little spots, much like a Dalmatian, over the rest of his whitish body. Appropriately, Snow tagged him Patch.

Of all the dogs Snow owned, he rated Patch as the most versatile, a once-in-a-lifetime dog. Patch could retrieve ducks as well as any Labrador, point quail as if he'd been born to it and work sheep like a true-blue champion. Snow believed his collie blood was the reason for this intelligence. Dog, Murray Ball's lovable Footrot Flats creation, would not disagree with that. Unlike his good-natured mother, however, Patch had one major failing — he was extremely aggressive.

'One day Colin lost his watch on the hill and we went back to try and find it,' explained Snow. 'He had a fair enough idea where it had happened and when we got there he looked at Patch and said "Fetch!" So Patch fossicked around in the tall grass and soon found it.

'Handle sheep? Listen, we'd shear, oh, thirty-thousand-odd ewes in three sheds down south and he'd pen the lot on his own!

'Fight? Shit, he was in at the drop of a hat. I mean, he used to get stuck into all of the dogs on the place I sheared on. In the end, he got that way that if someone strange went into a pen, he'd yank hard at their trouser leg just to let them know he was there.' Snow laughed. 'Course, a lot of cockies didn't take too kindly to that type of carry on and some of them kicked him in anger and he'd bite them back. And if he couldn't do it then, he'd wait until the right opportunity presented itself. He must've bit damn near every cocky I ever worked for at one time or another.'

'Did he ever bite you?' I asked.

Snow nodded.

'And?'

'Only once.'

For a good number of years Kim and her son, Patch, hunted together, the mainstay of the pack. Today, Snow is well aware that he'll never have it so good again. The years went by, the hunting was good. Patch was ripped from time to time, bruised a lot, but nothing he couldn't shake off like a bout of flu.

In the winter of 1983, when Patch was thirteen years of age, Snow was crutching on Kaiwera Downs, near Mataura, in Southland. Pigs were plentiful on the station and often after work Snow and one of his shearing mates would go and get a pig for tucker. On this particular evening, they went to a rough block, all fern and scrub on the steep side. According to the owner, Ivan Dickie, a formidable black boar had taken up residence there and had already given one hunter's dogs heaps.

Formidable, the way it turned out, was an accurate description of the black boar on Kaiwera Downs. For openers, he stood three feet high at the shoulder, measured seven feet in length, and weighed around 310 pounds. To top it off he was armed with knife-edged weapons that protruded a good 3½ inches. He looked like a direct throwback to the European wild boar. He was a magnificent specimen.

Snow's team of dogs soon caught up with the big black boar, for he resided in a comparatively small area. When Snow and his equally breathless mate put in a belated appearance it was all on. The sheer size of the demented boar, plus the fact that at least one of his dogs was badly ripped, made Snow realise that the sooner it was over, the better. He whipped his .303 to his shoulder, but the dogs were hanging on to the boar for grim life and there was no way he could be sure of the shot. He had yet to hit one of his dogs and today was going to be no different.

With amazing agility the boar jack-knifed, the dogs only just hanging on. Then the boar broke free of most of them. Tusks flashed, a dog screamed, another flew through the air for several metres before the boar, with a powerful lunge and a deep snort, powered off through the dense fern. The dogs did not pursue him; they had all been ripped or badly knocked about.

The next winter Snow Quinn and his team of shearers were back on Kaiwera Downs. Same old crutching. It paid the bills. The big black boar was still there. It had been quite an eventful year: he had killed several dogs, ripped many more, gored two men in the legs. He had gained a fair amount of notoriety in the district. He dearly loved a good scrap and would wait in ambush for the dogs, then, as they approached, he would charge at them. Because of his great strength, weight and determination, there was no way dogs could hold him. One thing was certain: there was no way he was about to quit his territory.

The challenge the big black boar presented was, of course, difficult — if not impossible — for Snow Quinn to ignore. Several times he tried his luck, but each time events followed a similar pattern: the dogs got on to the boar, there would be a short but frantic confrontation, and before Snow got there he was gone.

By this time, Patch was fourteen, and his reflexes were not as sharp as they'd once been. Even so, he was still keen; he always would be. Still, Snow knew it was time he was retired. It was time to take life easy on a farm in the south; he had earned it. What happened to Patch the next time the dogs encountered the big black boar made Snow wish to God he'd already pensioned him off.

The big black boar was gone and the dogs were a beaten lot. The same old story. But Patch was more than beaten — Patch was done for. There was a deep gash in his chest, a horrendous tear that extended from one shoulder, across the back, and right down the far leg. He might have been whacked with a well-honed scythe. As best he could, Snow patched the wounds. Then he carried him out to his Land-Rover. Early next morning, he took Patch to a local vet, who could only marvel that the dog was still alive. It would take fifty-four stitches to hold Patch together.

'Somehow he pulled through but that was really it for him. He spent the last four years of his life on a farm down south. He did a little duck-hunting and sometimes worked stock in the yards; I think he enjoyed himself well enough . . .' There was a faraway look in Snow's eyes, more than a hint of sadness in his voice. Old Patch.

Yet Patch lived on in a way, for Sam was his son and would display many of his father's outstanding traits but, fortunately, none of the aggression.

In June 1988 Snow Quinn was back on the familiar turf of Kaiwera Downs. The black boar was still firmly entrenched there; he saw himself as a part of the station. Pig-hunters still tried their luck, Ivan Dickie got it right when he said to Snow one day, 'I don't know where all these dogs are coming from because he seems to be killing them off quicker than they can breed them!'

The boar was responsible for the death of many dogs, certainly in double figures, which would be reason enough, you might think, to leave him well alone. Try telling that to a diehard pig-hunter like Snow Quinn!

So, five years to the month after he first hunted the boar, a never-say-die Snow Quinn was back in his territory. He had five dogs: Sam, Spot (Sam's mother), Major, Bess, and a young bailer. In the gloom of evening, the dogs were barking like crazy in an isolated patch of second-growth bush. Snow, above them, moved quickly, throat already dry. Too late — the boar was off. Gone down-gully. Behind were two lightly ripped dogs. Not again, Snow groaned inwardly.

He is still unsure what happened next. The boar apparently ran as far as a small creek, which Snow had crossed a short time ago, and then turned about and ran back the way it had come. Snow believed that some of his scent must have remained on the ground and the boar, heading into the wind, had smelled it. The boar, possibly confused now as to precisely where the danger lay, ran into the path of Sam and Spot. They bailed him up in deep cover only a short distance from Snow.

The rest of the dogs rushed past Snow and into the fray. The barking reached a high-pitched and fearful level. They wanted help — and yesterday! But Snow was unable to see the boar. Damn the poor light! Below him, looking up with pleading eyes, was the young bailer. Already ripped, his message was obvious: do something, anything!

And then Snow's penetrating gaze came to rest on a large dark object about 50 metres away. Was it the boar? Then it moved a little, and the sound of tusk on grinder was all Snow needed to raise his rifle.

Careful! Spot and Sam were close to it, hemming it in. Willing the round home, Snow aimed at what he thought was the boar's huge head. The light was so poor he could hardly make out the foresight. The sound of barking was suddenly obliterated by a booming crash. On Kaiwera Downs in the gloomy evening one more wild pig fell victim to the good old .303 calibre.

Buster

It was a beautiful June day in 1991 and I was with Colin and Judy Ashmore in the lovely old cottage that goes with the job of stationhand on Murray McMillan's property. Looking out from the station flats, as I had earlier paused to do, had revealed a lovely view on an equally lovely winter's morning: mist trailing the winding course of the Clutha River, and, beyond, on the eastern side of the valley, the sun flooding the rock-strewn hills of Bendigo and Northburn stations, glittering on the frost-tipped grass.

Colin is in his early forties, a little over average height and solidly built with an easy-going nature on the hill. I suspect strongly, however, that it would be a mistake to rub him up the wrong way. He's a diehard pig-hunter. Born in Southland, he had been on Mount Pisa for nearly five years; he reckoned he'd taken twenty boars and heaps of smaller stuff in that time.

The sport is not without its dangers on Mount Pisa station. In May of that year Colin and Ray Buchanan, a shepherd on Northburn station, had gone hunting on Mount Pisa's southern boundary with Waitere station — great pig country. Soon they found sign of a big boar; Colin wondered if it was the same animal that he had been in contact with some time before. That one was living much higher than here — up around 1000 metres, say — but the spot was still pretty much in a general line with where they were now. He put voice to his thoughts and Ray, curious, asked him to explain further.

Colin said that he had shot a large number of goats that had apparently wandered onto the station from another run. A boar had quickly found the carcasses; moreover, he had set up camp above them in snowgrass country. His den, Colin added, pointing, was way up there on a sharp ridge that captured the sun early on and, come evening, was reluctant to surrender its warming rays. The only way you could have found the den,

Colin reckoned, was the way he had: by more or less stumbling upon it. Ray asked if he saw the boar. Colin replied that he hadn't.

They did not see a boar that day.

During the following week, Colin's work took him to the same general area where he and Ray had seen the big tracks; again he saw the same-sized spoor. One evening, mid-week, he told Murray about it and said that if there wasn't much doing on Saturday morning, well, he'd like to have a crack at getting it. The boss was all for it; controlling pigs was by this stage part of everyday station life on the Pisa Range.

Saturday morning, around dawn; a heavy frost, looking real good. In low gear, Colin's beat-up Land-Rover ground slowly up a steep, slippery slope. On the open back of the vehicle were six caged dogs. One of the eager dogs was Buster.

Buster was something of a comedian, into everything. There was something very special about Buster and the entire family had warmed to him very quickly. Buster received preferential treatment: on birthdays and at Christmas he was allowed to come into the house and share in the festivities. Great for Buster, but not so good for the rest of the dogs as they, drooling, listened to Buster's account of meat and gravy and heaps of spuds and Christmas pud.

It was lighter now. Colin's companion on this particular day was Gary Bright, Murray's son-in-law. Gary was looking forward keenly to what lay ahead. The boar, providing they could get onto him, should provide great sport. Presently they reached the newly formed track and Colin drove slowly along it. Suddenly, he slammed on the brakes.

Gary gasped, 'What the ——'

But Colin, yanking open the door, was already outside.

'Look here!' Colin said, kneeling. With a stabbing forefinger, he indicated fresh pig tracks. Big pig tracks. 'The crafty bugger came along here last night after I knocked off.' He chuckled softly, picturing the boar hunting for worms and what-have-you in the newly turned ground.

Quickly, Colin freed the dogs. They tumbled out of their cages in their haste, some to pee, others to sniff the ground. Not so Butch — the ace finder was off; soon the other dogs followed him. With rising impatience the men waited to hear a tell-tale bark. At last it came, a distant sound, beyond a number of ridges.

The boar had finally been bailed three ridges away from where he had foraged on the track. He was in a dank little creek that in winter only briefly saw the sun. It was little more than a muddy watercourse overhung with ferns. The boar was ginger and black, strongly built and agile on his feet; at around 240 pounds on the hoof, he was in prime condition. Add to this a ferocious nature and sharply honed tusks, and he just had to be bad news. He had not liked being disturbed, and he hated dogs.

By the time a puffing Colin reached the creek, he had left Gary, who was having difficulty with his footing on the icy ground, far behind. A horrendous sight met Colin's eyes.

'Oh, no!' he groaned.

Buster was down, lying motionless on his right side as the churned-over water lapped around his muzzle. Colin winced; he knew that Buster was done for. He was either dead or very close to it. He had been gored only once, but it was enough. A deep hole had been punched in his chest, severing a major artery. Buster had, in all probability, drowned in his own blood. Shaking, Colin reached for the sheath knife at his hip. A life for a life? By God, yes!

Meantime, the other dogs were giving their all: Mate was hanging on to an ear; the young Rhodesian ridgeback, Zeus, was gripping a back leg; the others were mixed in there somewhere. All the dogs and the frenzied boar were covered with blood and muck. All but the Rhodesian ridgeback were wounded — cuts, rips, jabs — and Butch had fared the worst.

With the utmost care, Colin moved in behind the boar and deftly used his knife. The blade went in deep behind the boar's shoulder, the entire blow struck with tightly controlled fury. By the time Gary arrived it was all over.

Colin, grim-faced, oddly reticent, was checking out a whimpering Butch's wounds — a deep gash across the middle of his back, throat torn open, numerous small razor-like cuts.

'Shit!' Colin muttered.

Still Gary took in the scene. Great sport? No, he thought not.

Colin moved on to Patch and saw that he had been ripped across the belly and the bulging grey sack of his intestines was starting to press through the slit in his soft skin. What about Buster? It was better not to dwell on him, Colin mused. The pig-hunter's eyes misted over. How was he going to tell Judy?

While Gary stayed with the dogs, Colin ran back to the Land-Rover and drove it up, very close to where Buster lay. Very gently, Colin placed Buster's body in the back. The rest of the dogs seemed to be in shock as they entered their cages. There were no winners today on Mount Pisa station.

Later that day Gary Walker treated to Colin's wounded troops at his veterinary surgery in Wanaka. It took three hours to attend to them all. Gary considered that Butch was lucky to be alive and, while the dog was unconscious on the operating table, he showed Colin where the boar's tusk, in neatly slicing the throat, had actually grazed the jugular vein.

Hard Action on Queensberry Ridges

'More coffee?' Judy asked me.

'Sure, thanks,' I replied, thinking about the story Colin had just told me. It's never easy to lose a good dog, whatever the reason.

'So how are the dogs now?' I said, turning to Colin.

'Good as new.'

'Even Butch?'

'Yeah, even him.' Colin smiled. 'He hasn't been out after a pig since then, so you can bet he's rarin' to go.'

'And what happened to Buster?'

'Buster?' Colin paused and stole a look at his wife. 'He's buried out there in the garden.'

'We miss him very, very badly,' Judy said.

'Yeah . . .' Colin agreed.

The silence was heavy. I doubt very much if the Ashmores will ever forget Buster.

Colin shrugged away the nostalgic talk of Buster and, putting down his empty coffee cup rather noisily, got up from the table and left the room. In his absence, Judy and I chattered away like a couple of magpies. Presently, Colin returned, dressed for the hunt, Winchester .30/30 in hand.

'May I . . .?'

'Sure,' Colin replied, handing me the rifle, butt first.

'Belongs to the station,' Colin explained.

I nodded. 'Been around, I'd say.'

'And then some.'

The Model 1894 had a steel buttplate, which indicated it wasn't new. By its serial number, I judged it to be of pre-1964 manufacture. After 1964 this and other Winchester models were put together in Japan, which not only turned collectors of Winchester firearms right off but also resulted in poorer workmanship.

'Ready?' Colin asked.

'As I'll ever be.'

'Good.' He turned to Judy. 'Might be back in time for a late lunch.'

Judy smiled; she'd heard that one before.

In perfect conditions, we put Mount Pisa station behind us, heading north along State Highway 6, destination Queensberry Ridges station. When pigs had been liberated on Lochaburn station in the late 1970s, Queensberry Ridges station hadn't existed. It sprang to life in about 1982, when the 4250-hectare Lochaburn run was split up, with Geoff Brown retaining the homestead and Denis Fastier taking control of the 1600-hectare northern block, which he named Queensberry Ridges. Interestingly enough, it was on the northern block that pigs had first been liberated.

Only weeks before Colin and I arrived on Queensberry Ridges one June mid-morning, Denis Fastier and Jane Stevenson, the woman he lived with and who helped run the place, had been mustering a hill block (they are all pretty much hill blocks there) when their eight sheepdogs had taken off after much meaner game than hoof-stamping merinos. The object of the chase quickly turned and backed into heavy manuka. Now get me!

Breathlessly, Denis and Jane arrived to find their dogs facing a decidedly irate pig. A big pig at that, with a very scruffy black-and-tan coat. Before they were able to determine the sex the pig broke and the dogs, at Denis's heated command, did not pursue it. Not that Belle, a huntaway bitch, would have wanted to give chase, you understand, she was badly distressed, having been badly gored. Off for treatment to Richard Bishop in Cromwell, then.

Denis also wasted little time in informing Colin Ashmore about what had happened to Belle, and precisely where it had taken place. Colin set out with his dogs and caught up with an animal that perfectly matched the description Denis had given, very close to where Belle had been ripped. It was a sow armed with very small but very sharp weapons. As a matter of interest, a couple of local pig-hunters examined Belle's healing wound and pronounced that, because it had been a substantial injury (requiring stitches on the inside, too) a sow could not have caused it. I have no doubt whatsoever that a sow could have inflicted such a wound: it's not the size of the tusk that matters, but how sharp it is and how it is used.

I was mulling this over as Colin and I cut across a flat paddock towards the foothills, where a number of goats were grazing. They were a part of a 2000-strong herd that Denis, back in the days when goat farming had seemed the answer to a runholder's prayer, had gradually built up. Today, he might have been pushed to even give them away.

Colin had told me earlier that a large black boar had been seen on several occasions on Queensberry Ridges. Now wouldn't it be really something, I thought, if we saw him today? Wouldn't it make for high excitement and hard action?

An hour later, heart pounding, I snapped to my eyes my 7 x 35 field-glasses as the sound of Patch's barking, throbbing with urgency, came from the lower slopes of a deep gully. There!

A brownish boar was exploding out of a patch of towering snowgrass. He weaved between two thick patches of manuka with the dogs in hot pursuit. Mate was up front and Patch close behind; the rest of the six-strong pack did their best to keep up. Down through the scrubby growth the boar ran, churning up clouds of fine snow as he skidded past a clump of speargrass. The boar powered downslope, but the dogs were closing the gap.

Below, Colin was snaking through tall stands of dead manuka. They had had a burn-off here and the manuka were still mostly standing, their skeletal limbs tempered by fire to form formidable weapons that could easily blind a careless hunter or rip the soft skin of a dog in pursuit of a pig. With ease, Colin clambered onto a flattish outcrop of rock, the better to see. Motionless, he watched the action.

Still the boar ran full tilt. Ahead of the fleeing pig a small creek fought its way through the thick snow. Not breaking stride, the boar crossed it with ease, then barrelled across a snowy face. The chase continued across that pristine white sheet, the boar stretching out, chunky legs a blur. Yet somehow Mate had narrowed the gap even more.

A far bigger creek, the main one in the gully, lay directly ahead of the boar now. It was choked with all types of vegetation, mostly bent under snow. Beyond the creek the country was steep, a hillface in heavy shade. Faster and still faster went Mate, now grabbing at the boar's shoulder, failing to make hard contact, a scrape of teeth on hard hide.

Suddenly the boar altered course, kicking a flurry of snow into Mate's face, and headed down into the creek, out of sight. The dogs followed and a single triumphant bark rang out. There was no sunshine where the boar, grunting madly, faced his uncompromising enemies. Boar and dogs played out a grim drama with one inevitable conclusion: death.

Within sound of the creek it was bitterly cold, the ferns bowing under the weight of icy snow. The creek was like gunmetal, with a small series of rapids and smooth rocks coated with thick ice. The dogs were holding the squirming boar when Colin and I linked up with them. None of the dogs appeared any the worse for the encounter; I was more than a little thankful for that.

With a look of great satisfaction, Colin went in to despatch the boar. It was all over, but for a few minutes the creek ran red. The dogs still hung on to the boar as though he were alive.

'Get outta there!' Colin snapped and, with reluctance, still caught up in the heat of battle, the dogs backed away. Then Colin smiled at them.

'Good dogs,' he praised. 'Good dogs.'

Kneeling, I took a close look at the boar's tusks: they were long, well shaped, thick at the base and virtually unmarked. They were magnificent tusks, the best I had seen in a very long time.

'Top trophy!' I said.

'You're not wrong,' beamed Colin.

'Gonna take the jaw?'

'You bet!'

I nodded at the dogs. 'It's a wonder they didn't get ripped, eh?'

Colin inclined his head in agreement.

Meantime, the dogs stood pretty much together, shivering violently, Patch most of all. A hot shower and a brisk towelling down would have him fixed, no worries.

'You can't always see a wound at first glance, y'know,' said Colin. 'The one that did old Buster in was no more than a finger-sized hole — all the damage was internal.'

'Like a high-powered bullet,' I offered.

'Yeah — like that.'

Carefully, like a monkey examining the coat of its companion for fleas, Colin checked out each dog in turn. They stood patiently while he poked about. They liked his touch and his voice; they would have died for him. Pig-dogs are like that.

'Hey, not a single graze,' Colin said, relieved.

'Just as well.'

Colin raised his eyes. 'Don't remind me! Buster was the fourth dog I've had killed by a boar. That's four too many. Don't want it to happen again. . .' A bleak look stole like a black cloud across his ruddy face.

Up in the sunlight, I photographed Colin with the boar and had a strong feeling that I had the cover shot for this book. Then we headed up with curiosity to where we had first observed the boar breaking from cover; Colin's angle was completely different to mine, of course.

The boar, we realised, had been in his den when the dogs had disturbed him. It was a fine spot, obviously picked with care. He had constructed a scooped-out hollow on a narrow bench and lined it with grasses and ferns. It was directly below a clump of thick snowgrass, which formed a sort of roof. There was heavy cover on three sides of the den, so that a silent approach on foot would have been impossible. Indeed, you could have been standing only a metre from the boar and, unless he had moved, you would have never known he was there. The den was positioned to take full advantage of the sun.

Kneeling, I looked more closely at the nest; I felt the sun-warmed grasses and ferns, and found a few crinkly body hairs in the bedding. Typically, it was not soiled in any way. I smelled the grass and fern and the odour of the now-dead boar, a warm and live smell. Not too long ago he had been here, enjoying the sun, not bothering anyone or anything. Less than an hour ago he had been here, I thought, and a wave of sadness engulfed me. I started after Colin Ashmore, realising I was getting more sentimental the older I got.

No real distance from the boar's den, and directly uphill, was a sow's nest. She had formed with her snout a roundish hollow in which there was ample room for both her and her young. The den was below a very low-growing live manuka, and the branches made the nest virtually waterproof. On this bright afternoon the sun was flooding into it. I had been up with the Queenstown birds and, after a hard slog up the hill, I could quite easily have stretched out for a few hours' sleep myself. Can you imagine the sow's surprise had she returned to find me sleeping there?

Colin was checking out the nest too, looking for tracks. 'She must've been here when we got on to the boar.' He nodded uphill. 'They took off up there.'

Meantime, I had noticed that the nearest droppings were six or seven metres away. Dirty pigs?

Glancing around, Colin said, 'Where the hell is Butch?'

The answer was obvious: he had taken off. Like Buster, Butch was a finder and a holder. Now that Buster was only a memory, Butch was Colin's only far-ranging finder. It's not really fair on any dog to be left to cope single-handed if, say, it got on to a really dangerous boar. On the other hand, a team of good finders and holders could together contain even the meanest boar.

Again like Buster, Butch was not without personality. He was the type of dog that pig-hunters talk about together, the stories often humorous, sometimes chilling, invariably interesting. In the December of 1990, Colin had gone hunting with his two teenage sons, Richard and Tim. They had driven to the top of the Pisa Range, which is not as difficult as it sounds: there are a number of tracks. The day turned misty in the afternoon, but they had already caught three good-sized pigs. Two had been dumped in the back of the Land-Rover and the other, too knocked around by the dogs, had been left behind. Butch had taken off along the top of the range after another pig.

Hours later there was still no sign of Butch. By now the mist was even thicker, and the temperature was falling by the minute. There was a chance of snow, so they returned to lower ground. Colin was convinced that Butch would trail them home.

A week later Butch hadn't turned up. Then a tramper called in at Mount Pisa station, and said she had seen a lone dog right on the tops and did they know of anyone who had lost one? Soon, Colin was heading high. Right on top of the range, he came across an unperturbed Butch. He was very well conditioned — he had been feeding on the carcass of the pig. He had been in a fight, too: a few pokes here and there, the odd patch of skin off, all healing nicely.

'Funny thing,' Colin said, 'was that he didn't really want to come home with me. He seemed quite happy living up there all on his own.'

'As long as the pork lasted,' I pointed out.

'Dunno about that,' Colin said. 'He's quite capable of fending for himself.'

So Butch had disappeared again. On a distinct spur, we paused and looked to the valley of the Clutha River, with Cromwell away to the south-east. It was, by any reckoning, a fantastic view.

Faint . . . yes . . . barking. Good old Butch. What had he found?

Colin turned to me, smiling. Together, we moved quickly, while the dogs sprinted ahead. We headed downhill fast, through soft, powder-like snow.

'Hey!' Colin called over his shoulder. 'Pigs were up here recently.'

Sure enough, you could see their tracks in the snow. There were lots of tracks, left by a family of pigs; over there it looked like they had rolled in the snow like big kids. The ground shelved away, a wide bench, the land falling sharply beyond it down to the scrubby creek. Colin, talking rapidly, told me he had just seen a pig moving from left to right across a manuka face directly below us.

'Big pig?' I asked.

'Uh-huh.' Colin's eyes narrowed. His face was thoughtful, maybe a little puzzled.

'Boar?'

'Yeah — a big black bugger.'

'The one that ——'

'Reckon so,' he replied flatly.

I moved a short distance away to get a better view. Suddenly I could see what Colin couldn't — a big black animal skylined and then, just as suddenly, lost from view over a low ridge. I moved back to Colin and told him. He removed his green canvas hat and ran his fingers through his hair. He replaced his hat, then tugged at one end of his 1970s-style moustache.

'Must've broke on them, I reckon.'

'Nothing new, is it?'

'It is with my dogs. Once they've bailed a pig, well, that's usually it.'

'Buster wasn't there, was he?' I pointed out thoughtlessly. 'That could make a difference.'

'Hmm . . . you're probably right there.' But something was happening down below that was not to Colin Ashmore's liking.

To complicate matters further, the dogs put in an appearance on the same slope where we had both seen the boar. They were not trailing it, but were rushing about in circles like gutshot roos. They didn't seem to have a clue about what was going on when, in fact, they should have been hard on the boar's heels.

'For fuck's sake!' Colin muttered darkly. 'Listen, I'm going to cut down here. You head back to that ridge.' That would lead me close to the Land-Rover. Colin set off at a jog.

For a few minutes I glassed the dogs and saw them settle down and then follow the boar; I watched them drop one by one over the same ridge the boar had vanished beyond. I started upslope. The snow was knee-deep, clinging and incredibly tiring. The smudged tracks of a hare indicated it had gone uphill too. You can be quite sure it made much easier work of it than I did. On the ridge proper I paused, heart hammering, in dire need of a knee replacement. There were more hare tracks here, going this way and that. Two animals, maybe. Snow is great fun if you're fitted out with big, paddle-like feet that in a pinch would substitute for skis.

With the Land-Rover in sight, I checked out the hillface opposite me and the tracks of the boar — clear-cut in the snow — seemed to leap up at me through the field-glasses. I followed the tracks to where I had last seen the boar and, for that matter, the dogs.

Surprise!

A pig had topped the ridge in very much the same spot the black boar had crossed it ten or fifteen minutes ago. It was not a black boar, either. It was, in fact, a dead ringer for the one Colin had taken earlier, the same offbeat shade of dun colour. Maybe he was a brother or cousin.

I paused to refocus the glasses. The boar dropped down off the ridge and was difficult to pick up once he entered low cover because of his camouflage. Then he was in the snow again, clearly visible. He was a good-looking animal, rather chunky, like an All Black prop.

I heard barking, then I could see dogs on the skyline. The boar lunged into a run, heading downslope, and after him went the dogs. Way above, Colin hollered out; lifting my eyes, I spotted his ant-like form on a rocky knoll. The boar, predictably, was bailed in a creek.

Colin made his way down the tricky hillface. All the time the dogs were barking and the boar carried on as though demented. Standing there, merely a spectator with no say in the outcome, I longed for an end to it. Soon it came — a long drawn out and quite horrendous death scream.

A little later Colin appeared below me, the boar on his back. The gutted carcass was about equal in weight to the live weight of the other boar, around 150 pounds. With a look of pure relief, Colin dumped the boar on the ground near the Land-Rover. He wiped his hand across his perspiring cheeks, allowed a flicker of a smile to cross his mouth, and said with a heavy sigh, 'Doesn't get any easier, does it?'

'Don't ask me — I'm out of practice.'

He laughed. 'Make a heap of sausages out of this one,' Colin said, jerking a thumb at the carcass. He stretched his back slowly, working his solid shoulders; he didn't have to tell me what the carry up from the creek had taken out of him. 'See the black boar again . . .?'

'No. You?'

'Uh-huh.' He cast an eye at his dogs. 'Got a strong feeling they didn't want to have anything to do with him, you know.'

'How d'you mean, Col?'

'Butch got ripped up again.' Colin groaned.

'Poor little bugger,' I said as Colin displayed Butch's wounds. They were not pretty; large patches of skin had ripped clean away and were simply hanging in bloody flaps over the red raw meat. Butch stood there stoically, possibly in shock.

'The vet's for you, my boy,' Colin said at last.

We prepared to leave, wondering which boar — the big black one or the tan-coloured one — was responsible for goring Butch. We reached the conclusion that the black one had ripped up Butch and that the scenario had been something like this.

Butch would have bailed up the black boar and, without his longtime mate Buster, it had simply proven too strong and too determined for him to cope with. Consequently, he had been knocked around. The boar had broken on him before the other dogs had arrived. We had, of course, seen the black boar making good his escape. Butch? He was still smarting from being roughed up by an expert, and was reluctant to give chase. It was common sense; a pig-dog can only take so much. Later, and after some confusion, the dogs had bailed up the tan boar.

There was one thing that backed up our theory: the tusks of the dead boar were blunt, round and smooth. With 150 pounds behind them they could, of course, have jabbed deep into the hide of any dog, but they couldn't have made the neat, surgical slices of Butch's wounds.

We could only speculate. Butch, of course, lying down in a woebegone manner, knew all the answers.

A Life in Your Hands

Some pig-hunters, not wanting to incur a vet's fees, might have attended to Butch's injuries on the hill or when they got him home. Colin Ashmore, however, while well capable of stitching up wounds, was taking no chances. A very precious life was in his hands. Butch didn't seem to be too badly injured and yet, as Colin pointed out to me again, it is often impossible to know when a dog is injured internally. That was for an expert to decide.

Dr S. G. Mirams — Steve to his mates — is a Wellington-based veterinary surgeon who specialises in home calls. Steve knows all about injured pig-dogs and the Khandallah Veterinary Clinic even offers a special discount to members of the fast-growing Upper Hutt Pig Hunting Club. Steve has some pithy advice on the subject of first aid for dogs. He recommends that pig-hunters carry with them a first aid kit containing, at the very least, sutures, needles, a bottle of disinfectant, antibiotics, bandaging and a tube of antibiotic cream or powder.

If one of your dogs gets severely injured you should clear the airway, check he is still breathing, control the bleeding and look for a heart beat by placing your hand over his lower chest. Remember that an injured dog is frightened and disoriented — approach calmly and restrain the dog if necessary.

The best way to stop bleeding is to apply pressure over the area. If you're carrying a suture kit, and the wound is not too large, sewing the wound may help until you can get to a vet. Some pig-dog injuries result in damage to arteries, particularly in the lower legs and chest area. If the bleeding is uncontrolled the blood loss can lead to shock and death.

Shock is the loss of blood supply to important body tissues, and it can be so severe that the dog dies quickly, particularly from a severe wound. The symptoms of shock include lethargy, very fast breathing and shivering. If the dog goes into shock it is very important to restore the blood pressure. Stop the dog from moving — carry him out if you have to. Stop any bleeding if you can. On leg wounds and some body wounds apply a pressure bandage; for larger body wounds, hold something clean against the wound until you're out of the bush. Try and relieve pain — pain makes the shock worse — and give the dog suitable antibiotics if you have them. Don't give the dog food or water.

The next step is to get the dog to the vet. If the dog has part of his gut hanging out or a wound into the chest it is very important that the exposed tissue be kept as clean as possible. The more infection gets in, the less likely the dog is to recover.

If you have got a suture kit and the wound is small enough, you can fix it yourself. Make sure the wound is clean — if you haven't got disinfectant, heaps of clean water will do. Use a sharp blade to scrape the edges of the wound; this will help the wound edges to heal to each other. Apply the sutures so that the wound edges just touch — the suture does not have to be tight. The dog should be given antibiotics for at least four days. If the wound is not dry and clean within thirty-six hours, contact a vet.

When recovering from injury or anaesthetic your dog needs warmth and will sleep a lot, so bedding should be dry and out of the way of draughts. Very restricted exercise is recommended for the first few days; rest is important to avoid stress on the wounds and suture lines. Long runs should be avoided. Your dog's recovery will be quicker if he gets small meals at regular intervals, as large amounts of food at one time probably will not be tolerated. Your dog may not get his appetite back for several days after anaesthetic. Lots of water is also important.

Butch was in the back of my hatchback and we were close to the lovely little township of Wanaka now. Wanaka, so different from glitzy Queenstown, is more like the New Zealand of the 1950s and 1960s. To the west of State Highway 6 the northernmost peaks of the Pisa Range fell away to stock-dotted hills, to the north-west were Mount Aspiring and the Matukituki Valley, and away to the north-east was the rugged landmass that forms the spinal column of Mount Burke and Glen Dene stations.

Very little wild pig control work happened on both of these stations during 1991. Naturally enough, it did not please either of the runholders in question. According to Paul Hondelink, policy dictated by the powers that be in Wellington was the main reason why they hadn't been able to sustain hunting pressure. Another significant reason was that neither station was on DoC land and the Department was primarily concerned with its own land.

Hondelink and Fleming have noticed a gradual increase in pigs on both stations, and that they are already moving back into favoured foraging grounds. They were back to square one.

Those who call the shots at the Department of Conservation head office, but do not fire the shots on the ground, do not rate wild pigs as a serious threat; they rate feral goats, possums and thar as more of a problem. I can't argue with goats and possums being on the list, but thar? Thar are one of the world's great trophy animals, which, if handled correctly, will prove more of an asset than a liability. Unlike wild pigs they really do need protection.

Colin Ashmore flashed a look over his shoulder at Butch.

Keeping my eyes on the road, I said, 'How's he doin'?'

'Looks OK — not too distressed, I guess.'

'Can't say the same for you.'

'Can't help worrying,' Colin said with a shrug of the shoulders.

A short time later, Colin told me to take a right turn to Gary Walker's place.

'This must be like old times for you.' I couldn't resist that.

'Huh?' Colin was obviously thinking about something else.

'Going to see the vet again so soon.'

'Shit!' Colin moaned, 'I can live without that!'

Maybe he was already thinking how much this particular trip was going to cost.

Aspiring Veterinary Service is on Andersons Road, tucked away from downtown Wanaka in a back street. Typical Central Otago suburbia. While Colin went inside to get Gary, I flicked open the hatch and went around to the back of the vehicle.

'Hey, boy!'

Butch looked up.

'You'll be a box of birds soon,' I told him. Of course, Butch may not have wanted to be a box of birds.

I stroked his muzzle and he licked the back of my hand with great care; there was trust in his dark brown eyes. I was glad we hadn't let him down. Moments later Colin and Gary Walker, a slim, personable type, came into view and Colin introduced me to the smiling veterinary surgeon.

'Only got one for you this time, Gary,' Colin said, reaching into the back of the vehicle and gathering Butch very gently in his strong arms. Butch did not resist.

Soon, an unconscious Butch lay outstretched on an operating table. Gary and his no-nonsense assistant, Ros Moseby, worked quickly, expertly, and with grave concern for the wounded pig-dog. Lion-hearted Butch was in the very best of hands.

Butch was fully recovered from his dust up with a boar on Queensberry Ridges station within a week. He couldn't wait to get back on the hill again — much like his master.

These two symbolised to me the continuing saga of pig-hunting in this country: a sport, a necessity, even a way of life. Colin was simply following his basic instincts to hunt. Without this essential hunting instinct the human race would not have survived. Even those who today decry hunting, often with good reason, would, if circumstances demanded, take up a weapon and hunt to survive.

Butch had been bred to hunt and trained to hunt. That was his role in life. He didn't question it but revelled in his unique lifestyle.

The big black boar that had gored him still ranges Queensberry Ridges station and the adjacent runs; Denis Fastier tells me that there are times when it seems there are no pigs on his place and then, suddenly, they are back in force. I would have dearly loved to have seen this particular boar at close range — not to see him killed but simply because it would have brought me into real contact with a prime example of perhaps the most adaptable animal in the world.

In Closing

It is a particularly lovely mid-morning in Queenstown. The sun is flooding my office and I can hear on a light breeze the song of a bellbird. I pause to collect my thoughts. What, I wonder, is the black boar doing right now? Perhaps he is in his well-chosen den, soaking up the sun of the first fine day in well over a week. Perhaps he is thinking about gooseberry bushes loaded with soft, yellowing fruit, one of the joys of summer. Maybe thoughts of a saucy young sow living a few scrubby gullies away cross his mind.

More likely he is sleeping. Yet even in slumber he is aware, a certain part of him switched on to the possibility of danger. That marvellous sense of smell, far beyond the comprehension of a human being, will warn him should an enemy approach upwind. His highly developed sixth sense will make him snap fully awake in a fraction of a second if, suddenly, all is not as it should be.

Yes, a truly splendid wild boar inhabiting an equally splendid mountain range in Central Otago where, until the late 1970s, there were no wild pigs at all.

Bibliography

Books

Animals of Moorland and Forest, Orbis, London, 1970.

Barnes, F. C., *Cartridges of the World*, DBI Books, Northfield, Illinois, 1980.

Brander, M. (Editor), *The International Encyclopedia of Shooting*, Pelham Books, London, 1972.

Bucher, R., *The Book of Hunting*, Paddington Press, New York, 1977.

Burton, M. & R., *The Animal World*, Macmillan, London, 1977.

Donne, T. E., *The Game Animals of New Zealand*, John Murray, London, 1924.

Fraser, C., *Beyond the Roaring Forties*, Government Printing Office, Wellington, 1986.

Glover, H., *A Standard Guide to Pure-Bred Dogs*, Macmillan, London, 1977.

Holden, P., *The Wild Pig in New Zealand*, Hodder & Stoughton, Auckland, 1982.

Holden, P., *The Hunting Experience*, Hodder & Stoughton, Auckland, 1988.

Hunting, Nordbok, Sweden, 1980.

McCaskill, L. W., *Molesworth*, A. H. & A. W. Reed, Wellington, 1969.

Mochi, U. & Carter, T. O., *Hoofed Mammals of the World*, Lutterworth Press, London, 1974.

Newton, P., *Big Country of the South Island: North of the Rangitata*, A. H. & A. W. Reed, Wellington, 1973.

O'Connor, J., *The Big Game Animals of North America*, Outdoor Life, New York, 1961.

Reid, J. W., *Pigs*, Farmers & Stock-breeders Publications Limited, London, 1955.

Reader's Digest Book of Facts, Reader's Digest, New South Wales, 1986.

Reader's Digest Complete Book of New Zealand Birds, Reader's Digest, New South Wales, 1985.

Ricciuti, E., *Wildlife of the Mountains*, Harry N. Abrams, New York, 1979.

Wild Herds, Time Life, 1977.

Wild New Zealand, Reader's Digest, New South Wales, 1981.

Wises New Zealand Guide, Wises Publications Limited, Auckland, 1987.

Other Sources

Barron, B., *Pig and Goat Survey: Pisa Range*, NZFS, Queenstown, 3 August 1984.

Black ice on streets before respite arrives and *Shotover River freezes from bank to bank*, Southland Times, 18 July 1991.

Chamberlain, L., *Wide interest in pig-hunting contest*, The Press, 13 October 1990.

Clarke, C., *Can Hunters Control Feral Pigs?*, paper presented at Seminar 2000: Wild Animal Management, NZDA, Christchurch, 1988.

Feral Pig Control Handbook, Queensland Rural Lands Protection Board.

Feral Pigs and their Distribution, Bulletin of the Queensland Rural Lands Protection Board, 1987.

Feral Pigs/Tuberculosis in Wild Pigs, DoC/MAF, 1985.

Grady, D., *Wild porkers for the pot* and *Cyril's heyday as a hunter*, Weekend Star, 28 May 1988.

Hondelink, P., *Illegal Pig Liberations: Minaret Station, Lake Wanaka*, DoC, Wanaka, 6 June 1989.

Hondelink, P., *Pigs: Albertburn — Craigieburn — Makarora*, DoC, Wanaka, 5 February 1988.

Hondelink, P., *Wild Pigs: Mount Aspiring National Park*, NZFS, Hawea, 12 July 1982.

Hondelink, P., *Wild Pigs: Mount Burke Station*, NZFS, Hawea, 12 July 1982.

Huge boar fights to death, Southland Times, 24 October 1990.

Matthews, K., *Release and Establishment of a Feral Pig Population in the Kaitake Range*, DoC, New Plymouth.

Martin, R., *Feral Pig and Goat Populations: Pisa Range and Tarras Areas*, NZFS, Queenstown, 30 June 1982.

Martin, R., *Pigs: Liberations*, NZFS, Queenstown, 7 May 1985.

Martin, R., *Pigs: Pisa Range*, NZFS, Queenstown, 30 June 1982.

Martin, R., *Pisa Pig Survey*, NZFS, Queenstown, 10 August 1982.

Miscall, P., personal diary, 11 June 1990 to 3 September 1990.

MPs favour myxomatosis, The Mirror, 23 January 1991.

Orwin, J., *Pig Hunters and their Dogs*, Rod & Rifle, September/October 1990.

Orwin, J., *The Forest Institute report on hunting in New Zealand*, Rod & Rifle.

Pig claims perplex researcher, The Dominion, 11 August 1988.

Pig hunters raise TB concern, Waitomo News, 15 March 1990.
Pig pest raises hackles, The Press, 21 July 1990.
Pigs off to Market, The Star, 28 May 1988.
Pittaway, B., *Grandad*, Rod & Rifle, May/June 1987.
Rabbits lose ears to cold, The Press, 12 August 1991.
Rigby, S. C., *Mt Pisa Survey*, NZFS, Queenstown, 28 February 1985.
Teamwork bags huge boar, Southland Times, 6 November 1990.
Unusual boar close to extinction, NZPA-Reuter, 1986.
Wild pigs top mercury levels, The Star, 2 December 1987.